KIDS
who outwit adults

John R. Seita and Larry K. Brendtro

Foreword by Matt Damon

Solution Tree

Published by Solution Tree (formerly National Educational Service)
304 West Kirkwood Avenue
Bloomington, Indiana 47404-5131
(812) 336-7700
(800) 733-6786 (toll free)
FAX: (812) 336-7790
e-mail: info@solution-tree.com
www.solution-tree.com

All *Good Will Hunting* quotations in this book come from either the
videocassette (1997. Produced by Lawrence Bender.
Directed by Gus Van Sant. 126 min. Miramax) or the screenplay
(Matt Damon and Ben Affleck. 1997. New York: Miramax/Hyperion).

This book contains numerous quotations by and about troubled youth.
Many of those quotations contain profanity. In an attempt to avoid
particularly offensive terms, some words were partially replaced with
hyphens. For the most part, however, the content of these quotations
remains unchanged.

Edited by Sandra L. Knauke
Cover design by Grannan Graphic Design
Text layout by Maria McGrorey
Production assistance by Kimberly Harris

Printed in the United States of America

ISBN 1-932127-32-1

We dedicate this book to the resilient young people

who shared their personal worlds with us.

About the Authors

John R. Seita, Ed.D., overcame a troubled childhood to become an expert on resilience and positive youth development. Currently, he is on the faculty of the School of Social Work at Michigan State University where he also has appointments with MSU Extension/4-H and with the Michigan Agricultural Experimental Station. He is also an adjunct professor with the School of Child and Youth Care at the University of Victoria in Canada. Dr. Seita worked for five years as a program director for the W. K. Kellogg Foundation in Battle Creek, Michigan. Previous appointments include director of program evaluation for the Kalamazoo County Human Services Department, program administrator for the Calhoun County Community Mental Health Department, and research associate and adjunct professor at Western Michigan University. He began his career as a direct care worker with troubled youth in correctional and treatment settings.

Dr. Seita's first book, *In Whose Best Interest? One Child's Odyssey, A Nation's Responsibility*, relates his own experience of overcoming adversity and provides a model for building resilience in schools and communities. *God is in the Kitchen and Other Everyday Miracles: A Daughter's Gift and A Daddy's Love* is an inspirational collection of reminiscences and lessons learned in the parenting encounter between father and daughter. He also is editor of a monograph on resilience, *Celebrating Survivors*. Dr. Seita has written extensively in various journals on subjects related to positive youth development and program evaluation. He speaks widely to audiences of professionals and community leaders on principles of positive youth development. Dr. Seita attended Western Michigan University, receiving his bachelor's degree in sociology, and his master's and doctorate in educational leadership.

Dr. Seita is married to Lori, and they have a daughter, Anorah.

Larry K. Brendtro, Ph.D., is former president of Starr Commonwealth, which serves troubled youth at campuses in

Michigan and Ohio. He is founder of Reclaiming Youth International, a nonprofit organization linking professionals, policy leaders, and citizens concerned with troubled children and youth. He has been a youth worker, teacher, and psychologist. He taught in the area of behavior disorders at the University of Illinois, Ohio State University, and Augustana College. His doctorate from the University of Michigan is in education and psychology, and his dissertation focused on youth with problems of conscience. He has over 120 publications and is coeditor of the quarterly journal *Reclaiming Children and Youth*. He established the Black Hills Seminars, an international training institute, and has trained youth professionals worldwide.

Dr. Brendtro's books are available in several languages and include *The Other 23 Hours*, *Positive Peer Culture*, *Re-educating Troubled Youth*, *Reclaiming Youth at Risk*, *Reclaiming Our Prodigal Sons and Daughters*, and *No Disposable Kids*. Dr. Brendtro is a member of the American Psychological Association and holds a federal appointment on the Coordinating Council on Juvenile Justice and Delinquency Prevention chaired by the U.S. Attorney General.

Dr. Brendtro and his wife, Janna, have three adult children and divide their time between Michigan and the Black Hills of South Dakota.

Table of Contents

Outwitted

He drew a circle to shut me out,

Heretic, rebel, a thing to flout.

But love and I had the wit to win.

We drew a circle that took him in.

Edwin Markham
(1852–1940)

Foreword

by Matt Damon

This is a book about healing and relationships. It is based in a fundamental belief that every young person has the capacity to find connection and meaning in life; it is about our potential to grow and change even under the worst of circumstances.

I grew up with what John Seita and Larry Brendtro call "family privilege"—the invisible package of assets that provide a child with a sense of belonging, safety, unconditional love, and spiritual values. When I was small, I had the luxury of spending what I remember as most of my time imagining, making up stories, and play acting scenes that I invented. I didn't have to worry about my safety, about hunger pains, about where my mother was; I didn't have to be on alert for signs of danger. I was free in every way to play, imagine, use my toys and costumes to act out whatever scenarios I could dream up. Opportunities to discover my interests and talents with the support of a secure and loving family continued throughout my childhood and youth and set me up for life. My own accomplishments are as much a product of the unearned privileges John and Larry describe as they are of my own effort and talent. If my life circumstances had been different, I am sure I would not be writing the introduction to this fine book right now.

In our screenplay for *Good Will Hunting*, Ben Affleck and I created the relationship between Will Hunting and his therapist, Sean. We never imagined that this drama might later be used to help troubled kids like Will transform and heal. It is exciting and humbling to see how our work has been applied in a whole new direction for the purpose of helping young people.

Will Hunting easily could have had a different life path. Without Sean's belief in him, Will likely would have been diagnosed with antisocial personality disorder and sent to prison as a high security inmate. But Sean puts the strength-based interventions described in this book to work with Will. Holding onto his belief in him, Sean is finally able to establish a human bond with Will that transcends his fear of rejection.

The positive treatment interventions described here have changed the course of many lives that were headed down a self-destructive path. From a place of love and a belief in young people's capacity to grow and change for the better, John and Larry show us how to connect to recalcitrant youth, how to get on the same side of treatment with them, and how to work with and not against them.

John Seita and Larry Brendtro use the story of Will Hunting as a springboard for a new approach. They give us a detailed understanding of how we can and should shift efforts to help young people from a model of blame and pessimism to one that embodies hope and a positive belief in others. It seems to me that particularly in these times, when so many children and youth suffer from the various forms of violence that pervade our culture, when we hear loud calls for harsher discipline and punitive measures to control young people, we need the insights and wisdom offered in this book.

Movie as Mirror

Stories of youth battling adults are among the most powerful themes in literature: The prodigal son defies his father; Romeo and Juliet deceive their parents; Huckleberry Finn tricks his foster mother and rafts away on the river. The advent of motion pictures brought new heroes in the war between generations. *Rebel Without a Cause, West Side Story, Dead Poet's Society, Girl Interrupted*, and *Good Will Hunting* all show conflicts between adults who want control and youth who want independence.

This book is based on the real-life stories of young people who are stunningly skillful at outsmarting adults. Our inspiration for this project was the movie *Good Will Hunting*, written by Matt Damon and Ben Affleck, who earned Academy Awards for their fictional screenplay. They also performed the roles of Will and Chuckie, friends growing up together on the challenging streets of South Boston.

Will Hunting is distrustful and defiant. Early abuse and abandonment have left him raging against his rejection. Longing for love but fearful of being hurt again, Will is on guard against people who get too close. He battles anyone who tries to control him. After outwitting a string of court-appointed therapists, Will is sent to Sean, an unconventional psychologist played by

Robin Williams. Sean refuses to be driven away by Will's hostility and searches for the good in this troubled but talented youth.

Upon first seeing *Good Will Hunting*, we (the authors) spoke on the phone. We were struck by the similarities of the movie to our own early, turbulent encounters. The two of us also began as adversaries: John Seita, an angry and adult-wary boy; and Larry Brendtro, a psychologist, frustrated in his attempts to reach him. Our paths first crossed in 1967 at Starr Commonwealth, a residential program for troubled youth in Albion, Michigan. John Seita came to Starr under court order; Larry Brendtro came under contract as the new president of Starr. Today, we are friends and professional colleagues.

We have used scenes from *Good Will Hunting* in our work to connect with young people and to train youth professionals, parents, and civic leaders. While writing this book, we met Dr. Nancy Carlsson-Paige who teaches at Lesley University. In a case of remarkable serendipity, we learned that she is not only an expert on violence in children and conflict resolution, but she is also the mother of Matt Damon. We greatly appreciate the interest and encouragement that Nancy and Matt have given to our project.

This book explores the *private logic*[1] of kids who battle adults, and it provides a blueprint of practical strategies for connecting with and reclaiming them. We have drawn from our own experiences in youth programs, gained over many years spent on one side of the desk or the other. We reinforce key ideas with stories of conflict and survival. These stories capture the courage of the human spirit. They jolt us into awareness of new truths and point the way for overcoming life's challenges.

Each chapter in *Kids Who Outwit Adults* is introduced with a segment from the story of John Seita's own journey from risk to resilience. Drawing from our research and practical experience with youth issues, we then offer our perspectives on the themes in John's story. The scientific foundations of this work come from exciting new knowledge on positive youth development, also called positive psychology, strength-building, and resilience. The focus of positive youth development is on developing potentials instead of dwelling on deficit and deviance.

The most powerful voices in this book are those of youth. We went straight to the source to interview real-world Will Huntings. We found them in schools, juvenile facilities, and treatment programs. They came from inner-city Detroit, the suburbs of Chicago, the villages and reservations of the heartland, and the streets of Sydney, Australia. We sat in barren cells with homeless street kids, and we spoke with youth of privilege who came from mansions without love. In many ways, they were all the same. They identified with the adults-as-enemy view of Will Hunting. In the words of seventeen-year-old Nathan, who had been brutalized in a string of foster homes: "Watching *Good Will Hunting* was like seeing my life pass in review." As they recount how they fight the adults who pry into their private worlds, some of these youth show a sense of pride. Others speak with shame, for the wounds of rejection run deep. But beneath their bravado or reserve, all are longing to find someone worthy of trust.

Every citizen shares the responsibility of creating communities in which all young people can thrive and grow. Whether we serve as mentors, teachers, counselors, parents, pastors, or policy-makers, we must learn to understand and connect with our youth. Both adults and young people must gain the courage to put down their armor and join in an alliance.

Endnotes

[1] This term was frequently used by Alfred Adler. 1930.

chapter one

Angry and Defiant

The first thing that happened to him was that he was abandoned by the people who were supposed to love him most.

—Sean Maguire, Will Hunting's therapist, *Good Will Hunting*

I too was abandoned. Many times. For the most part, I grew up without the privilege of a family. My mother gave birth to me when she was only seventeen. Records show that she had few parenting or job skills, lacked personal maturity, and may have been a victim of abuse herself. I was too young to really understand what her pain may have been. My mother's background is documented in my case history:

> *It is not known whether or not John's mother finished high school. She came to the attention of Juvenile Court authorities when filed on by the Board of Education for incorrigibility. She first ran away from home when she was thirteen years old. A psychiatric evaluation at that time recommended placement for*

intensive inpatient psychotherapy. However, she remained only two weeks and ran away.

Mom's troubled life didn't get much better. She was married at least twice as a teen and later had two more children: my half-brother, Jimmy, and half-sister, Maria. When I was five years old, I watched my mother's current husband relentlessly beat her. During an argument at dinner, he exploded at her and nearly jumped over the kitchen table. He grabbed her by the hair, pulled her from her chair, and banged her head repeatedly against the kitchen wall. Even now I can hear the thump, thump, thump of her head bashing the wall. After only a few seconds of this beating, I saw blood gushing from her head and splattering on the wall. She pleaded that she was "seeing stars." I remember her screaming that he may as well go ahead and kill her. Then he abruptly stopped beating her, loaded us all into our old blue Pontiac, and drove to the hospital emergency room.

When I was six, my mom tried to commit suicide and was sent to a psychiatric hospital. After she returned home, she and her husband separated multiple times. It was disturbing and troubling for all of us. After several years of conflict, they divorced. Thereafter, my life took a turn for the worse, if one can imagine that.

Ours was a world of poverty, alcoholism, deprivation, decay, and the madness of the inner city projects. Our little family moved around more than anyone I knew because mom couldn't pay the rent. I would rather not remember any of the places we lived, but I do. They were smelly, filthy, vermin-infested, and falling-down decrepit. Often our utilities were disconnected, and we went hungry. A report in my case file reads:

> When the Women's Bureau investigated the home, there was no food; there were broken beer bottles strewn on the floor, and the place was in a state of utter dishevelment. The mother had been leaving the children unsupervised most of the time. The children were all very undernourished.

It was easy to see that my mother was not prepared to care for us. She exhibited poor judgment in many ways. I was walking *alone one day, a seven-year-old, trying to escape the apartment and its madness. An old, rusty, barely road-worthy car pulled up next to me on the curb. The occupants, a seedy-looking bunch with yellow teeth, leaned out of the windows and ordered me into the car. I refused and started to run, but one guy jumped out and grabbed me by the waist. He forced me into the car and threw me into the back seat. "Where do you think you are going, little man?" this frightful man jeered. I bit his arm. He smacked me across the mouth. He told me that they knew my mom and that she had asked them to pick me up. They were complete strangers to me, and I had never seen them or their car before. Fortunately, they took me to my mom's apartment. That night, my bed was the floor, covered with my mom's coat. I fell asleep to the sounds of yelling and breaking glass.*

When I wasn't home, the streets were nearly as scary. There was no safe haven. By the time I was eight, I had been mugged twice. Both incidents were terrifying. The first time, I had walked down dark and abandoned streets late one night to the grocery store to buy some potato chips. Grabbing a small measure of joy, I walked along eating them. Suddenly a teenager attacked me. He brandished a knife, held it menacingly near my chest, took my chips, and threatened me if I told anybody. I thought he would stab me, but he didn't. I ran home terrified. No one was there.

The second time, I was taking delight in jumping into slush puddles. Nearby was a house rumored to belong to an actor who had played a role in a popular movie. I wondered why a famous actor would be living in my part of Cleveland. Still, the possibility was pretty impressive to me. Then, it happened. A group of four older boys knocked me on the ground, pummeled me, and pushed my face in the snow. They stuffed snow inside my pants and coat. I kept hoping for the "famous actor" to come to my aid while they were beating me, but he did not. He waited until after they were gone and then came outside to see if I was OK. I remember thinking that he was a coward for letting me get hurt and doing nothing until it was too late. That was the story of my life.

Each day was filled with risk, fear, loneliness, hunger, and a lot of confusion. Safety was a constant concern. Although I don't remember serious physical abuse, the threat of harm hung every-where. We were largely unsupervised. Mom was either gone from our apartment or bringing home a string of men and wild friends. I often hid in the corner of the apartment to stay away from flying beer bottles. A social worker wrote in a report: "Mother gave very poor care to the children: they often went unfed, they were frequently left alone. She had no qualms about bringing her gentlemen friends for fun and games to the apartment where she had the children."

On what I felt was the worst day of my young life, my mother took us three kids with her in a dirty cab to the court building in downtown Cleveland. She said she had to talk to a judge and told me I was the oldest and should watch over Jimmy and Maria. Some social workers whom I had never seen before took us to sit on a wooden bench outside of the courtroom. A few minutes later, I heard my mother screaming, "No, no, no, no, no!" I ran to the room and looked inside to see who was hurting her. I saw her rolling around on the floor, crying, "I love my babies, please don't take my babies away!" I tried to rush to her aid, but the workers restrained me. I never lived with my family again.

Families on the Edge

Modern society is producing packs of kids detached from adults. Some roam wild as "mall orphans," while others are banished from our schools and communities. Children who do not bond to a caring adult come to believe they are unwanted and unlovable.[1] The result is anger and aggression, often mixed with shame and depression. They target their rage at adults, who failed to meet their need for love, and at themselves for not deserving that love. Defiant and distrustful, they are society's unclaimed kids. They are forever biting the hand that didn't feed them.

Troubled behavior results when children are deprived of the ingredients for positive development. In a healthy family, children receive emotional nurturing and guidance. In a healthy school, supportive teachers instill academic and social competence. As youth gain independence, healthy peers provide belonging and positive values. The broader community also provides healthy support and standards through churches, employment, and social organizations. These positive connections protect youth against a wide range of risks. But broken bonds or a lack of these positive connections produce what Lisbeth Schorr calls "rotten outcomes."[2]

In the movie *Good Will Hunting*, Will Hunting is an unparented youth who grew up in abusive foster homes. He is ashamed of his background and hides it from his girlfriend, Skylar. Instead, he tells her that he has twelve brothers named Marky, Ricky, Danny, Terry, Mikey, Davey, Timmy, Tommy, Joey, Robby, Johnny, and Brian. He creates them to project the appearance of normality. Skylar confides that she misses her father, who died when she was thirteen, and would gladly trade everything that she has for just one more day with him. Will responds with "at least you have a mother."

We aren't told what happened to Will's family or why he is an orphan and so alone. Maybe Will's parents were killed in an accident. Perhaps his mother was a young, single parent who gave him up for adoption, or his parents simply got divorced and neither wanted Will. Maybe he was taken from his home due to neglect or abuse. Whatever happened, Will is deeply wounded, and his feelings of rejection ooze out of his very being. Will has experienced the deepest of human loss: he is missing the basic kinds of privileges that are provided by stable families and environments.

Family Privilege

We define *Family Privilege* as the benefits, mostly invisible, that come from membership in a stable family. Most people cannot even imagine what life might be like without Family Privilege. Only as we recognize the power of Family Privilege can we begin to grasp how its loss or absence hinders development. Bill Buford notes that family is the essential presence—the thing that never leaves you even if you have to leave it.[3]

Family Privilege is an invisible package of assets and pathways that provides us with a sense of belonging, safety, unconditional love, and spiritual values. With Family Privilege, children observe parents or older siblings to see the effort it takes to be successful in life. Family Privilege provides the chance to hope and to dream.

Parents who provide consistent affection and discipline foster the development of Family Privilege. A variety of stressors, however, can interfere with normal parenting and the growth of Family Privilege. These stressors include hurried lifestyle, work pressure, poverty, divorce, illness, disability, criminality, substance abuse, and physical abuse. Adults who are extremely stressed or who lack parenting skills cannot form the bonds necessary for their children to develop social skills, self-control, and conscience.

Economist Theodore Schultz coined the term "human capital" and rooted it squarely in the family.[4] Like financial resources, human capital accumulates over generations and is passed from parents to children. Human capital includes the social and educational skills that allow young people to follow rules, solve problems, and communicate at a high level.

Family Privilege is a form of human capital that compounds its benefits over time. However, large numbers of youth today operate without the support of stable parents, an extended family, or even minimal traces of Family Privilege. Even in traditional families, Family Privilege is not a given. It must be intentional, not simply hit or miss or hope and pray. Those of us with Family Privilege take it for granted. Family Privilege is like oxygen—we don't notice its absence unless we are suffocating.

Loss of Privilege

The idea of Family Privilege hearkens to Peggy McIntosh who coined the concept of "white privilege," which is strongly influencing multicultural understanding. McIntosh suggests that prejudice is more than active discrimination; it is also an undeserved status bestowed by those with unearned privilege. Powerful benefits come with membership in a dominant group. For example, men do not worry about the possibility of rape when traveling in a new environment, but this is an ever-present concern of women. In this nation founded by European Americans, few whites feel they risk rejection when they enter a typical classroom, but such stresses are common to those of other cultures. McIntosh provides the following example of how white privilege affects her life:

> I have come to see white privilege as an invisible package of unearned assets that I can count on cashing in each day, but about which I was "meant" to remain oblivious. White privilege is like an invisible, weightless knapsack of special provisions, assurances, tools, maps, guides, codebooks, passports, visas, clothes, compasses, emergency gear, and blank checks.

> Other examples of white privilege abound: If I am white, I can, if I wish, spend most of my time in the company of people of my race. I can be fairly sure that my children will not come home from school devastated by racial harassment. I can be pretty sure that my children's teachers will tolerate them without concern about their race. When I see police, I am usually certain that they are here to protect me.[5]

McIntosh suggests that we cannot understand the barriers faced by minorities unless we first understand the benefits of whiteness. Likewise, in order to understand the barriers faced by those without Family Privilege, we must first recognize the benefits that come to those with Family Privilege. Here are a few examples of what it might be like to grow up without Family Privilege:

- As a small child, when I call out at night, I cannot be sure anyone will hear me. The people who come and go through my house frighten me. I never know if tomorrow I will live in this same home. I can never be sure if there will be anything to eat.

- When I start school, my parents don't attend conferences with my teacher, and I would be embarrassed if they did. If

I am sick, they can't find my mother. There is no one to help me with my homework or even to wake me up on time.

- As an adolescent, I can't bring friends home without being embarrassed. When I get in trouble, no one speaks for me. It wouldn't matter anyway because people in authority like principals, police, and judges don't listen to or respect my parents.

- As a young adult, no one helps me plan for college and career. If life gets hard, I can't ask for a loan or move back home. I don't know my relatives or my genetic heritage, and I have no family medical history. I can never be sure that I am unconditionally loved.

Family Privilege is best secured in the family. When that is not possible, or even the best plan, then Family Privilege becomes a community issue. Peter Benson notes that "all kids are our kids."[6] As long as there are any children at risk, then all our children reside in *at-risk communities*. Ironically, those children who most need Family Privilege from school and the community are those who are the first to be expelled, rejected, or relegated to substandard services.

Those who thoughtfully examine their own Family Privilege may come to some disquieting conclusions. Perhaps their accomplishments are as much a product of unearned privileges and circumstances as of individual effort and capacity. Even goals and dreams may be the result of Family Privilege.

As a society, we place high expectations on young people for achievement and prosocial behavior. Establishing standards without understanding privilege and handicap, however, is like expecting all youths to run a 100-meter dash in twelve seconds. One runner must jump over hurdles, a second runs uphill, and a third attempts to run the race on crutches. Meanwhile, three other runners in the same race have a smooth, dry, obstacle-free track and come out ahead of the rest. We applaud the three winners and look down on the others as losers. Only as we recognize their individual obstacles can we remove those barriers or help the runners overcome them.

Conflict in School

Most people never get to see how brilliant they can be. They don't find teachers that believe in them. They get convinced they're stupid.

—Will Hunting's math tutor, *Good Will Hunting*

When youth lack Family Privilege, then schools, churches, and neighborhoods need to help fill this gap. Often that is not the case. Schools are better at pulling weeds than at planting flowers.[7] In many schools, sassy students are unwanted weeds to be rooted out and discarded. They bring problems, shifting to school the hostilities that began in the family or on the street. These students display self-defeating patterns of distrust and disobedience. Assuming the worst about adults, they are in chronic conflict with authority.

John Odney is a veteran coach and science teacher of thirty years who loves to work with troubled kids. Thus, he is assigned the high-traffic first period detention that nobody else wants. Mr. Odney sometimes welcomes kids to detention with a handshake and then, like a coach, helps them figure out how they got benched. One of his students, a high school junior named Cole, tells how he gets into trouble:

> I usually get the big cheese—suspension. Teachers hear about me before the class even begins, so I'm stereotyped right from the start. I walked into the room a half a step behind the teacher, and the bell rang right when I entered the room. At the same time coming in the other door was a straight-A student. The teacher told me to get a tardy. I tell her I couldn't get my locker open. She sells me to write it on my tardy slip at the office. Well, of course, I have a temper, and I tell her to go to hell! Now I have another office referral. I kind of kicked the door when I left, too. I was pissed—excuse my language—so I went to the office and complained. No

good. Down there at the office, it goes in one ear and out the other. They don't care what you say.

Cole seems to be using the wrong game plan, playing both defense and offense against an unfair world. Unless he can connect with a teacher like Mr. Odney, who can show him a better strategy, Cole will keep getting into conflict cycles. Cole is hungry for acceptance by adults, however, and has a clever sense of humor. Even though he met Mr. Odney in the detention room, he soon shouts greetings to his "favorite teacher" across the cafeteria. Some of Mr. Odney's colleagues shake their heads and think he is foolish to waste time on a student like Cole.[8]

Dangerous Schools

For students on the edge, schools can become islands of stability or arenas for battle. Research showed that a surprising number of students experience traumatic stress in school.[9] Most commonly, this stress was from peer intimidation, but it also involved humiliation from school staff. Even if subtle, rejection by teachers is very painful, as these high school students describe:

> *After I had my baby last year, there were some teachers who acted like I didn't exist. They seem nervous even to talk to me.—Sharese*

> *I was walking down the hall, and I said "hi" to Mr. Nilson. He looked at me and said, "Oh, you're still here. You haven't dropped out yet?"—Lincoln*

A participant at a California conference for school principals reported that in her school the most favored punishments are "unbelonging" interventions, which typically separate students from their peers. These interventions include ISS (in-school suspension), OSS (out-of-school suspension), and ASS (new to us, this was after-school and Saturday suspension). These practices may protect school order, but they also result in school failure and student dropouts. Some healthy schools attempt to institute inclusive discipline strategies, but many more schools use exclusionary punishments. Adult-wary youths see the exclusionary punishments as an attack or rejection and become more aggressive or withdraw from school and teachers as a result.

By about fourth grade, students who have experienced continuing conflict with teachers begin to adopt a "bad kid" identity. At this point, these students are rejected by prosocial youth and begin to gravitate to other alienated students. Martin Gold and D. Wayne Osgood call this "school-induced delinquency."[10] Ironically, the self-esteem of these students usually improves once they scale down their goals and don't have to measure up to school expectations.

School violence is often carried out by alienated students who seek revenge within the school.[11] In the aftermath of highly publicized school shootings, there has been a debate about whether to profile kids who might commit such crimes, just like the FBI does with mass murderers. Irwin Hyman and Pamela Snook, leading researchers in school psychology, contended that we should instead profile the dangerous schools that cause *school alienation*, which results in three different patterns of behavior:

1. **Oppositional defiant**: Students hate going to school, mouth off, pick on other kids, are quick to anger, and do whatever they want even if others don't like it.

2. **Avoidant hypervigilant**: Students are afraid of being hurt, avoid certain places or people in school, don't trust others, and are always on guard against disaster.

3. **Depressed/hopeless/suicidal:** Students feel ignored by family, are failing in school, and don't care what happens to them. They consider killing themselves or hurting someone else and have no goals or reasons for living.[12]

There are large numbers of alienated students in any school, and schools alone cannot be expected to solve all of their problems. Nevertheless, schools are responsible for whether alienated students will be exposed to positive or negative school climates.

In positive school climates, students feel that they belong, are treated fairly, and are respected. They see the enforcement of rules as fair and beneficial. Students experience low levels or an absence of sarcasm, ridicule, put-downs, and verbal assault from either school staff or peers. Although cliques are normal in adolescence, the school staff takes measures to minimize their impact and support outcasts. Bullying or scapegoating by either students or staff is strongly discouraged. Students eagerly anticipate attending such schools in spite of high academic expectations.

Negative school climates occur when educators view students and their families as adversaries rather than valued partners. Students see the school as rule-bound with discipline administered unfairly by adults who don't really care about them. These schools have high rates of verbal assaults on students in the classroom. Name-calling, scapegoating, and put-downs are common from both staff and peers. Such schools have high detention, suspension, and expulsion statistics. The emphasis is on punishment, not prevention. Students retreat into cliques, and the gulf between teachers and students widens. Such schools alienate students who, as a result, develop hostile and angry feelings toward the school, staff, and other peers.

Dangerous schools result when alienated students encounter negative school climates. Negative school climates do not exist only in deprived neighborhoods. Even schools in communities of privilege can be seedbeds for alienation.

Alternatives Leading Nowhere

We addressed a Texas conference on building alternative programs for reclaiming troublesome students. Next to the podium was an attorney who said that our presentation was interesting, but if schools wish to save resources, they could place disruptive students on homebound instruction (the effectiveness of which, of course, is directly proportional to the degree of Family Privilege). He then proceeded to teach administrators how to comply with the law but still get rid of the student.

How can students who can't get along in school learn social skills at home? How can a parent be expected to handle a student full-time if the school can't manage six hours? If a youth is dangerous, certainly the justice system should be involved, but that doesn't cancel the need for education. We told our Texas colleagues that if their state had to ration resources, then the most troublesome students should be at the front of the line because we have more to fear from their ignorance.

By default, schools that aren't creating positive climates are in the business of negative youth development. Bluntly, they are making delinquents. It may be easier to blame parents than acknowledge the school's contributions to student problems. Even if problems start at home, it is often school failure that sends students over the edge.

School success can alter antisocial trajectories. Unfortunately, students who most need a comprehensive school experience often receive an academically and socially inadequate education. We visited an urban area where at-risk students are banished to home-based instruction because of their behavior. One hour each week they come to school to review their lessons with a tutor. Students who show "progress" may earn the "privilege" to reenter regular classes. How many privileged students could survive on this anorexic educational diet?

With the advent of zero-tolerance approaches to school misbehavior, a large number of students are shunted to "alternative education." Innovative alternative schools can succeed with very difficult students, but some of these schools are only warehouses. We recently accompanied a colleague on a visit to a new alternative school operated by the local school district. Walking along on a brisk and sunny early Midwestern spring morning, we were filled with the newness of life, the rebirth of nature, and were looking forward to visiting the alternative school. Our eagerness was short-lived.

We descended several flights of stairs to the "classroom" in the bowels of a local recreation center. People traveling to or from their workouts walked by the classroom, rubbernecking to get a closer look at the students in the room. We entered to discover four students, two female and two male, slumped over on their desks, seemingly asleep. All were African American. Neither of the two teachers, both white, was certified to teach. There were scant books, materials, or curriculum. There were no criteria for the students to be able to return to the regular classroom. Cast-off computers without software were in a state of disrepair; they were simply heavy paperweights. A discussion with the teachers revealed that neither had much hope for the students and both actually expected them to fail.

In reflecting on this alternative that leads nowhere, we concluded that school administrators were trying to store troublemakers out of sight in the hope that they might go away. If their intent was to create delinquents, they were on the right track. Here was their six-point plan:

1. Isolate difficult students from the rest of their peers.

2. Put them into disintegrating and unpleasant surroundings.

3. Hold minimal behavioral and academic expectations.

4. Offer no real curriculum or instructional resources.

5. Assign the least-qualified staff to work with them.

6. Eliminate opportunities for belonging and success.

Success in life requires skills. Feeble alternative schools are deserts for youth development. Even a student who might complete such a curriculum would be cheated out of a real education. As Michelle Fine notes, some students choose to drop out of dysfunctional schools as a way of taking charge of their lives.[13]

At a California conference, teams of educators and students explored ways of reaching alienated youth. The dean of discipline from one school introduced us to the students at his table, including Isaiah. Awkward in his six-foot-three, one-hundred-twenty-pound frame, fourteen-year-old Isaiah was enrolled in a program for troubled students. He had been forced to attend the conference by his mother, who thought it would be good for him. As we began our presentation, he tried hard to appear disinterested, but he was soon captivated by our stories of resilient youth who had turned their lives around. The session ended with discussion. While other youth participated, Isaiah remained silent. Then, a veteran teacher with an edge of anger in his voice rose to declare that teachers were there to teach those who want to learn and shouldn't have to waste time on those who don't. Isaiah's hand shot up, and he rejoined, "Attitudes like that are the problem. What will happen to kids without hope if teachers lose hope in them?" The answer to Isaiah's question is obvious. Abandoned by adults, many students will search for belonging in the company of others like themselves, who are unattached to family or school.

Prisoners of Peers

And why does he hang out with his friends? Because any one of these kids would take a bat to your head if he asked them to. It's called loyalty.

—Sean Maguire, Will Hunting's therapist, *Good Will Hunting*

Peer influence is often seen as negative because it is such a potent force in the lives of young people. Peer bonding meets a powerful social need, and it is generally a positive process. Youth who have weak connections to family and school, however, are highly vulnerable to peer influence.

Cut off from family, teachers, and positive peers, all except the most troubled seek bonds with antisocial peers. These bonds usually begin in school but move to the street as youth increase their freedom from adult authority. At this age, many youth are accountable to no positive adults. Immersed in delinquent subcultures, they learn values and logic from their antisocial peers—and perhaps from exploitative, drug-involved, or criminal adults.

A youth alienated from home and failing in school probably has very low self-esteem. But making friends with compatible peers, even gang members or other outcasts, generally improves the sense of self-worth. Just because a youth has questionable peers does not mean that all of his or her values are antisocial. Ninety percent of delinquents have positive values and would like positive friends.[14] However, if these friends are part of a delinquent or drug culture, the youth is pushed towards high-risk behavior.

The values of negative youth subcultures are often at odds with adult values. Many troubled boys lack positive male role models. Mothers and female teachers then become examples of goodness. As a result, when a boy reaches adolescence, he is attracted to delinquent lifestyles to express his insecure manhood.[15]

Harvard anthropologist Walter Miller studied the values and belief systems of lower-class delinquents. He found that they had very unique thinking about trouble, toughness, smartness, excitement, fate, and autonomy.[16] While Miller described only poor urban youth, the mindsets he identified are common among all youth who are alienated from mainstream adult values.

Trouble is a major concern of people without much status, since a person who lacks influence will find any conflict with authority full of danger. Families in turmoil may define the goodness of a boy or girl as the absence of trouble—instead of the presence of positive behavior. A good girl is one who doesn't run around and get in trouble with men. A good boy is one who doesn't get in trouble with the police. Success at school means keeping out of trouble with teachers. Just avoiding trouble, however, is insufficient training for the challenges of life. In some peer groups, creating trouble brings status. A youth kicked out of class may strut with proud defiance. Some youth even brag about "doing time" in jail as if it were an Olympic event.

Toughness is both a survival value and a compensation for feelings of powerlessness and vulnerability. Youth demonstrate toughness with physical power, profanity, and fearlessness against great odds. A small youth who fights somebody stronger, even at the risk of being beaten, shows courage and "heart." A youth may purposely mutilate his or her body to prove indifference to pain. If toughness becomes an inflated value, then its opposite is abhorrent. Weak, timid, effeminate, or cowardly boys are sissies. Increasingly, tough girls also reject any hint of weakness since this makes them vulnerable to exploitation. St. Augustine wrote in his *Confessions* that as a youth, he engaged in all manner of delinquency to prove that he was as fearless as he supposed his comrades to be.[17] Centuries later, this toughness ethic persists in a "boy code" that requires aspiring to macho status. With this mindset, even talking about problems is admission of weakness, as twelve-year-old Alan explains: "I'll talk to Kevin about what's up with me, but only on the weekends away from school. If we talked about that kind of thing at school, people would say we're acting like girls."[18]

Art by Robbie, age 15.

Smartness does not refer to scholarship but rather the ability to con others, such as making money by exploiting fools. Shrewd and skillful verbal repartee is highly valued. Prominent examples from African American street culture are rap music and the mutual insult game called "playing the dozens," where youth typically insult one anothers' mothers. The ability to respond to stressful situations with humor is another example of smartness, which is also a mark of resilience.[19] People lacking in smartness are gullible, slow to respond, and humorless. They can't return clever counter-insults when verbally harassed.

Street smarts have little to do with school smarts. The idea that intelligence is learned in a classroom is heresy to youth who belittle the importance of school. Most adults seriously underestimate the potential of streetwise youth. When we encounter students whose case files have to be hauled in with a forklift, the file probably documents how many adults he or she has outsmarted.

Excitement has long been associated with delinquency. In 1909, Jane Addams noted that the main difference between delinquents and other youth is that the delinquents have "a greater spirit of adventure."[20] She also noted that early America was a coastal nation where youth found adventure by going off to sea. In Chicago of 1900, there was no ocean, so delinquents hung out at the railroad yards and created their own adventure. From juvenile court data, Addams documents delinquent adventures like stoning passenger trains, uncoupling train cars, setting fire to the grease in axle boxes, and derailing freight trains. Addams sought to tap, rather than suppress, this "spirit of youth" as she led the movement for urban playgrounds and recreation programs to prevent delinquency.

Other educators and youth workers also tried to tap this motivation for excitement. In the mid-1800s, some states outfitted ships so they could send their delinquents to become sailors. Unfortunately, in a navy comprised only of delinquents, mutiny was sometimes the highest adventure. These techniques have been revived in modern maritime, wagon train, and adventure education programs for troubled youth.

Thrill-seeking is common in many adolescents. Few adults crave the excitement of bungee-jumping towers, mosh pits, and mega-decibel concerts. Thrill seeking can reach epic proportions among wild youth. The quest for excitement and thrills is often correlated with conduct problems and finds its most intense expression among delinquent youth. Being daring is part of the job description for youth who make a career of defying authority.

Troubled youth use excitement for various reasons. Some are trying to self-destruct. Others are self-medicating, using excitement as an antidepressant. Others use thrills to block painful thoughts of conflict or trauma. For example, when Nathan began to think of his rejection in twenty-two out-of-home placements, he would go out with peers, steal cars, race them over curbs to make them airborne, and "see how much hell I could raise."

Peer groups greatly increase the quest for excitement as youths pump one another up for pleasure-seeking. Well-socialized youth spend several evenings each week with their families, but hanging around home is a boring activity for youth used to non-stop stimulation on the streets. For many of those who crave immediate gratification, traditional school is the ultimate boredom. Instead of being so quick to diagnose these students with attention deficit disorder, it might be better to talk about the school's curriculum deficit disorder.

Fate is a central focus to a person who feels that others control his or her life. When good things happen, it is luck; when bad things happen, it is an omen. If fate rules, one does not have to assume responsibility for changing. People who focus on fate are less likely to have a future orientation. They don't believe that events are predictable and controllable, so they live for the moment. Youth-work pioneer Anton Makarenko of Russia made planning for the future a central teaching objective with delinquents. He felt youth needed positive short-term, midterm, and long-term goals. Thus, children should be given some anticipated joy for each day. Then, they should be involved in planning exciting activities that will be weeks or months in the making. After they have learned that they can control their futures, they can start planning life goals, such as vocation or family.[21]

Psychologists study fate under the term *locus of control*. Those who feel in charge of their lives have an *internal locus* of control. Those who feel like helpless victims operate with an external locus of control. There is some adaptive value to blaming bad outcomes on external forces. This strategy protects the self-esteem of a person who believes "it's not my fault." Fate complements excitement because it gives permission to take great risks. As one youth told us, "You die when your time is up, so what is the difference?"

Autonomy is an innate drive in all humans, but it is usually balanced with a need for belonging. When asked whom they trust, delinquents frequently answer "myself." Past events have shown them that they cannot depend on others, who have proven to be dangerously unreliable. In an early study of children with weak consciences, we found that they resisted all external control. This resistance was not genuine autonomy since few of these youth showed responsible behavior. For example, when asked to complete the open-ended statement "When adults tell me to do something . . .," most youth respond with a variation of "I do it." But boys lacking positive ties to adults more likely responded in anger: "I don't do it. I hate having people tell me what to do." Of course, that attitude sets up youth for conflict with authority, and ultimately, others take charge of their lives.[22] Bill from Australia shared his own troubled experience, which showed an exaggerated need to prove that others cannot control him:

> My father committed suicide when I was eleven, and my mother married a man who terrified, belittled, and beat me. He called me a "no-hoper" and a "criminal bastard." I hated him. I hated my mother for marrying this man. And I hated my father for killing himself and leaving me alone. When I was in foster care, my foster parents beat me up too. I didn't have anybody, so even though I was small, I had to take care of myself. Whenever people tried to control me, I would tell them to "get f---ed." I was sent to counselors who asked about my family, and I told them the same thing. If cussing didn't work, I would throw a chair and that always made them go away. Then I was sent to a juvenile prison where we were forced to do hard labor. One day I started a riot by getting the other guys to refuse to

stand up when the guards ordered us to go to work. I got locked up for three more months but it was worth it. The other guys looked up to me, and I showed the guards that nobody could f--- with me.

Youth who are securely bonded to adults gain legitimate autonomy and are less susceptible to negative peer influence. But youth like Bill display a pseudoautonomy that comes when they are estranged from adults. They loudly declare independence from adults and then flock to a group of like-minded friends who totally control their values and behaviors. Having become willing prisoners of their peers, they can be easily lured into destructive behavior.

Pathways to Violence

Whatever demons must be raging inside of Will, he is taking them out on Carmine Scarpaglia.

He pummels the helpless, unconscious Scarpaglia, fury in his eyes.

—Screenplay, *Good Will Hunting*

Aggression is a normal, instinctual, protective survival mechanism. But aggression such as Will's is provocative, not protective; it has become a way of life. What causes a child to become violent without apparent cause?

Among youth most alienated from adults are those who live by the law of the streets. On the streets, survival means gaining respect by intimidating others. Lacking any faith in adult authorities, alienated youth believe they must take care of themselves. They adopt oppositional behavior that allows them to survive in violent neighborhoods.[23] They are ready to fight at the slightest insult. Winning any shred of respect is immensely important when so little respect is to be had.

Tragically, few youth gain respect from the important adults in their lives. Lacking the respect that they need and crave, troubled young people try to gain some control over their lives and their environment. In his book *Lost Boys*, James Garbarino writes:

> Some of these boys appear so tough on the outside. But when I get a glimpse of their inner life, I am deeply touched by their vulnerability and their pain, and I come to see their toughness as a survival strategy, as something that helps them get through another day.[24]

Children who experience abuse instead of love fail to develop adequate conscience and empathy for others. A youth in a program for juveniles who committed homicide said: "I came from a violent family, only knew how to express myself through violence. I didn't care about anybody. I would think only about what I would gain. I wouldn't feel anything."[25] Marty, a young man in a Midwestern prison, said: "It is not easy to feel somebody else's pain when your own pain has taught you not to feel anything. It is not easy to feel compassion for another when so few have felt it for you."

Overt, hostile acts are not normally a child's preferred coping strategy.[26] Fighting against others is an extreme form of coping used when other means are blocked.[27] From this perspective, rebellious and antisocial behavior can be seen as a valiant attempt to improve one's life, albeit using flawed tactics. Research on aggression shows pathways by which a child may, to use a term coined by Criminologist Lonnie Athens, become "violentized."[28] Following is our four-step synthesis of the pathway to angry and defiant behavior:[29]

Figure 1

Pathways to Violence

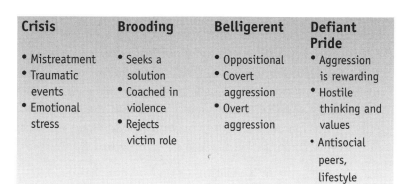

Crisis	Brooding	Belligerent	Defiant Pride
• Mistreatment • Traumatic events • Emotional stress	• Seeks a solution • Coached in violence • Rejects victim role	• Oppositional • Covert aggression • Overt aggression	• Aggression is rewarding • Hostile thinking and values • Antisocial peers, lifestyle

1. Crisis.

Children who have been ridiculed, rejected, terrorized, or traumatized can be overwhelmed by the extreme negative emotions of anger, fear, shame, and depression. Physical abuse, psychological abuse, sexual abuse, bullying, harassment, and neglect can cause children to believe that they are unlovable, powerless, and worthy of blame. Rejection can be as damaging as physical brutality. Love is the most powerful need of children, and love deprivation can create tremendous rage. A young girl describes her feelings of helplessness and fear:

> I tried stacking empty soft-drink cans by my bedroom door so I could hear when my stepfather came in the middle of the night. I tried to slide under my bed to hide, but he just threatened me and hurt me more. He said I was a slut, but if he got tired of my company, he would just go down the hall to visit my little sister's room. I knew Mother never would stop him, and I didn't think anybody would believe me. I was terrified.

2. Brooding.

A person who is unable to cope with stress is in a state of crisis and searching for a solution. The person considers possible scenarios and strategies in an attempt to stop the stressful situation. Some youth become depressed and wallow in self-blame; others become hostile and begin to fantasize ways of getting revenge. Violent thoughts are intensified by violence modeling and coaching from the attacker or others, such as "don't be a sissy; stand up and be a man." Athens offers this account of a young boy who contemplates revenge after being beaten by his mother for writing in a Bible:

> She took me in the bathroom and told me to take all my clothes off. I took everything off except my underwear. After she hit me with the belt three or four times, she said, "Take off your underwear, too." I said, "Okay, okay." Then she started slashing me all over my raw body. I screamed and screamed, but she wouldn't stop. It hurt really bad. I thought she was going to beat me to death. When I started crying and begging her to stop, she said, "You must be made to be sorry for the terrible thing you did so that you will never do anything like that again." . . . After she got tired of hitting me, which seemed like two hours, she opened the bathroom door. I walked out in a daze, completely naked in front of my sister. I had big blue welts all over my body. I felt completely humiliated as I walked up to my room. I lay on my bed crying and getting madder and madder. I looked out the window and saw the clothesline. I wished I could get that line and strangle her with it. I wanted to wrap that line around her neck and pull and pull and pull until I choked her to death.[30]

3. Belligerent.

While all children who have been hurt fantasize about hurting back, most don't follow through. They exercise self-restraint because of nonviolent values, fear, or a lack of opportunity. But with size, strength, and continuing provocation, some youth try aggression as a coping strategy. Deciding they won't take any more abuse, they choose a situation and a method to fight back. Examine the questionable success of a boy who was continually bullied on the basketball court and decided to fight back:

> I got mad and said, "Man, you better stop f---ing pushing me." He said, "F--- you." I waited for him to do it again. As soon as he did, I turned around and hit him four or five times in the face, which made him fall down. When he got up, he ran and grabbed a folding chair and hit me across the arms and face with it, which knocked me off my feet. I was lying on the gym floor almost knocked out with my face cut wide open and my eyes swelling up. I never really knew before how bad you could get hurt in a fight with somebody.[31]

Research suggests that youth show defiance using one of three major coping strategies. These include overt aggression (e.g., assault); covert aggression (e.g., vandalism); and oppositional behavior (conflict).[32] In a typical pathway, minor problems become more serious over time. Bullying expert Dan Olweus finds that many delinquents show behaviors from two or three of the pathways.[33] Aggression may be directed against an abuser or displaced on another target, such as a peer or less threatening adult. If violent behavior succeeds, it is likely to continue.

4. Defiant Pride.

If aggression doesn't achieve its aims, the youth will have to develop another solution or endure victimization. When aggression works, it can become a stable lifestyle. The youth becomes comfortable with violent behavior because it brings many benefits. The youth overcomes the initial crisis and, removed from the victim role, now feels comfortable, vindicated, and less distraught. In the individual's own mind, the power of bullying brings new status and perhaps inflated self-esteem. Any guilt about hurting others is managed by distorted thinking that justifies violence. Violence becomes fashionable as the youth cuts ties with prosocial peers and gravitates to peers who applaud this behavior—or to victims who tolerate abuse. Our culture provides abundant models for violence in the family, school, and streets. A teen shared this chilling account of violence as a virtue:

> After the stabbing, my friends told me, "Hey man, we heard about what you did to Joe. It's all over the school, everybody's talking about it. You must really be one crazy a-- motherf---er." My girl-friend said, "Wow, you stabbed that dude." Finally things came together and hit right for me. My girlfriend and all my other friends were impressed with what I had done. I didn't really care what my parents thought . . . nobody better piss me off any more unless they wanted to risk getting f---ed up bad. People were plain scared to f--- with me. My reputation was now made. I was in cloud nine. I felt like I had climbed the mountain and reached the top.[34]

In the pathway to violence, crisis situations can lead to patterns of coping behavior that persist years later. Though this behavior may appear maladaptive to others, it always makes some sense in the private logic of the individual.

Self-Defeating Strategies

Youth who show one problem are likely to have multiple problems. Thus, delinquency, abuse, drug use, sexual promiscuity, and school failure often go together. Some kids have psychiatric problems and become depressed or self-abusive. When working with young people, we find it helpful to track several parallel behavior pathways, such as histories of delinquency, drug use, sexual abuse, school achievement, and placement or treatment interventions.

Violence is but one of many types of destructive and self-defeating behavior. Psychologists have been very interested in tracking the pathways by which various problem behaviors develop. Some common childhood behavior problems develop, peak, and then decline. For example, telling lies often starts in early childhood, peaks after children start school and become more skillful at deception, and declines as they experience the results of dishonesty. Of course, some children keep lying until it becomes a lifestyle. Other problems follow different courses. Temper tantrums taper off after childhood, while drug problems increase in adolescence. On the other hand, positive events can encourage abandoning antisocial behavior.[35] While many factors predict problem behavior in a theoretical sense, all bets are off when it comes to one person and the private logic of that individual.

How do children and youth get locked in patterns of self-defeating behavior? We often ask young people: if you could go back and start your life over, how far back would you go? Most youth can quickly identify a specific point in time or a landmark event that put their life on a completely different course. Often it is a clear crisis such as the death of a parent or the day a father started abusing his daughter. If the question is phrased differently, young people also identify positive turning points. These might include finding a stable foster home, having a religious conversion, or participating in a treatment program. The impact of a landmark event is shown in this account shared by Brigit:

> Our family lived this idyllic life until I was fifteen. Then, one day when we were leaving for a vacation, my best friend, Randy, told me he was thinking of killing himself. I tried to cheer him up, and before we left we were joking around so I didn't tell anyone. But, as soon as we returned two weeks later, his mother came over to tell me the horrible news that Randy had committed suicide. "There was nothing anybody could have done; nobody had the slightest idea anything was bothering him," she said as we both cried. I felt Randy's death was my fault but told nobody. I began to drink and run

around with an older guy who had lots of problems. Sometimes I would go with him when he would break into stores and steal alcohol, but I told myself he would get into even more trouble if I weren't there; I needed to help him. When I did leave him, I got into relationships with other abusive guys. Eventually, I had substance abuse counseling and saw what I was doing to my life. I am now sober, have a great boyfriend, and soon will start college. I want to work with troubled children.

Perhaps the most telling information about patterns of self-defeating behavior in young people comes from listening to their own words and stories. The United States Secret Service studied the cases of forty-one children involved in school shootings over the period of twenty-five years. They read shooters' journals, letters, and poetry and interviewed ten of the shooters who sat for interviews in prison. These kids turned out to be more sad than evil. Luke, who killed his mother and two students in his Pearl, Mississippi, school, said, "It's real hard to live with the things I've done." Here is a glimpse of Luke's private logic drawn from an interview with a Secret Service agent:

Interviewer: Did any grown-up know how much hate you had in you?

Luke: No.

Interviewer: What would it have taken for a grown-up to know?

Luke: Pay attention. Just sit down and talk with me.

Interviewer: What advice do you have for adults?

Luke: I think they should try to bond more with their students. . . . Talk to them. . . . It doesn't have to be about anything. Just some kind of relationship with them.

Interviewer: And how would you have responded?

Luke: Well, it would have took some time before I'd opened up. If we kept talking . . . I would have . . . said everything that was going on.[36]

Reared in a violent culture, experiencing conflict at home and school, and perhaps ridiculed by peers, many young people do not have positive social bonds. As ties to families, communities, and the church weaken, our culture is producing a growing population of hostile, unattached children with weak consciences. The most seriously damaged youth leave a trail of broken relationships and see adults as enemies rather than protectors. Young people who most need trusting relationships with adults instead seek out other troubled peers. In the following chapters, we examine the dynamics that fuel hostile relationships. As we shall see, youth and adults who view one another as adversaries use remarkably similar defensive strategies of fight, flight, and fool.

Endnotes

[1] Bowlby 1982.

[2] Schorr 1989.

[3] Buford 1955.

[4] Schultz 1974.

[5] McIntosh 1995.

[6] Benson 1997.

[7] Eisner 1990.

[8] Odney and Brendtro 1992.

[9] Hyman 2000.

[10] Gold and Osgood 1992.

[11] Dwyer, Osher, and Warger 1998.

[12] Hyman and Snook 1999.

[13] Fine 1993.

[14] Gibbs, Potter, and Goldstein 1995.

[15] Cohen 1998.

[16] Miller 1958.

[17] St. Augustine [1923] 1959.

[18] Pollack 1998.

[19] Wolin and Wolin 1993.

[20] Addams 1909.

[21] Edwards 1991.

[22] Brendtro 1965.

[23] Anderson 1994.

[24] Garbarino 1999, 22.

[25] Matthews 1995, 11.

[26] Newman and Newman 1986.

[27] Balswick and Macrides 1975.

[28] Athens 1992.

[29] This is a synthesis of research reported by Athens 1992 and National Association of Addiction Treatment Providers 2000.

[30] Athens 1992, 34–35.

[31] Ibid., 66.

[32] Loeber and Farrington 1998.

[33] Olweus 2000.

[34] Athens 1992, 76–77.

[35] Rutter, Giller, and Hagell 1998.

[36] Dedman 2000, 8.

Rules of Engagement

If a patient doesn't trust you then they won't feel safe enough to be honest with you. Then there's no point to them of being in therapy.

—Sean Maguire, Will Hunting's therapist, *Good Will Hunting*

After the court took us away from our mother, I never saw my sister, Maria, again. My brother, Jimmy, and I were sent by the court to live in the Receiving Home. This big, gray, smelly, ramshackle building in inner city Cleveland housed kids nobody wanted. I couldn't believe how many other abandoned kids there were as we lined up nude to be issued our daily clothing. A profound loneliness for my family engulfed me. Religious scholar Stephen Mitchell describes being in love for the first time as a feeling so powerful that it is no longer inside of you, but you are inside of it. And so it was with my loneliness—I was inside of it, for years.

The first night away from our filthy apartment, I was angry, terrified, and unsure of what was going to happen next. Kneeling

*beside the rusty, metal-framed bed and urine-stained mattress, I
prayed to ease my pain. My cries for help felt like wails into an
empty universe.*

*After a few weeks, the court allowed Jimmy to leave the
Receiving Home to live with our dad. I still had hopes of return-
ing home, if not with my mother, at least with my father. Imagine
my joy when I was finally told, "Your dad is here to see you."
Seeking his embrace, I nearly sprinted down to the lobby. We
walked to his car. I sat proudly beside my dad on the front seat.
He was my hero who had come to rescue me from my captors.
He drove an old, rusty Mercury, but to me it was a carriage
worthy of a king. Together we went to a nearby drive-in for
hamburgers. My back was sore from stress and I sat stiffly. Dad
noticed and complimented me for being a tough little man and
not complaining about my pain. I was so proud to please him.*

*As we drove back to the Receiving Home, he said, "John, I need
to tell you something." I hoped he was going to say that I was
coming home with him and Jimmy. "John, you need to know that
I am not really your dad. I don't know who your dad is."*

*At first, I didn't believe him. Then my heart wanted to scream,
but I wouldn't give him the satisfaction. I sat stiff and straight,
and when the tears started to come, I turned away like I was
looking out the window. Not a word passed my lips. When the
car pulled up to the curb by the Receiving Home, I glanced out
the corner of my eye toward him. Our eyes never met. I strained
to push open the heavy car door with my shoulder and stepped
out onto the crumbling concrete. I walked slowly up the stairs to
the building; I wanted to give him time to call my name and say
he had changed his mind. No sound broke the night. My head
hung low. He was gone. Forever.*

*Pascal once said, "The heart has reasons which reason cannot
know." I didn't understand why I had lost my dad. But in my
heart I always knew that I had a mother. I loved my mom and
had tried to help her, especially when she was sick from drinking. When the court took her away, I begged for a chance to see
her, but they told me she was a bad mother and I needed to find*

a new family. I knew I had to prove them wrong: nobody would ever replace my mother.

Thus began my battle with every adult who entered my life. How could I—why should I—trust anybody? At the time, I didn't know that psychologists had stuck me with every diagnosis in the book. Some thought I was almost autistic. Others saw me as aggressive and hostile or manipulative. I acted all of those ways at times. I chose my behavior to fit the circumstances. Sometimes I sulked and withdrew. Other times I was angry and explosive. Most of the time I was sneaky. And, if it served my purposes, I could even be compliant. It was all a big game.

In many ways I felt that I was above consequences. There was nothing anybody could do to me that would be any more devastating than what had already happened. Adults tried to punish me into being the obedient young man they wanted me to be. Loss of privileges, isolation, spankings, and threats had very little effect except to solidify my belief that nobody could be trusted.

The Distrust Lens

Angry and defiant children often have a long history of unpleasant and painful experiences with adults. Even with well-meaning adults, a young person's emotional memory signals, "Don't trust this person or you will be hurt again." Viewing human encounters through the lens of distrust, they react with suspicion and fear. Once distrust is activated, humans are genetically programmed to respond with protective defense behavior.

In every culture, humans are hardwired to "do unto others as they do unto us." This is not the Golden Rule, but rather the *tit-for-tat* rule.[1] Most of us begin interactions with people in a positive manner but quickly reciprocate whatever we receive. Other things being equal, it is natural to treat friendly people kindly and hostile people with distrust and antagonism. Once, tit-for-tat had survival value by sorting potential friends from enemies. Such instincts are not well suited to modern urban life where we bump shoulders daily with hundreds of strangers.

Distrustful kids don't begin new relationships by giving others the benefit of the doubt. Assuming that others are their enemies, they are prepared for tit-for-tat antagonism. Well-meaning adults who encounter unearned hostility from distrustful youth often revert to the "normal" human response of tit-for-tat antagonism. Thus, distrust is like a perpetual motion machine. Adversaries become locked into self-perpetuating beliefs that are reinforced by the negative encounters they have with each other. As with family feuds, negative tit-for-tat can go on for years.

When criticism or control comes from people who are seen as cruel or rejecting, powerful negative tit-for-tat responses are triggered.[2] For example, nowhere is mutual hostility more obvious than in the tension between urban youth and urban police in the United States. A study of Boston police found that youth and police viewed each other with deep distrust. As community-policing approaches attempted to bridge the gulf between police and citizens, the distrust became apparent. In the eyes of the youth: "The cops are just a big gang—they don't respect the law, they cover for each other, they think they're all tough. They don't help us out." The view police held of youth was almost a mirror image: "We drive up, ask what's going on, and we get nothing but that tough-guy attitude. Then they blame us when one of their boys gets shot because we didn't keep the peace."[3]

Private Logic and Problem Behavior

What people think, believe and feel affects how they behave.

—Albert Bandura[4]

Based on critical life events, each of us has a unique view of the world. Alfred Adler called this unique view an individual's private logic—the personal perceptions and beliefs that strongly influence goals and behavior. Often, the only way to make sense out of behavior is to understand the person's goals, which result from private logic. Adler suggests that "when children make a mistake, it is because they have a mistaken goal."[5] Without information about the goal of the behavior, corrective efforts may not work and could cause even more problems

It is not so much what happens to people that influences their behavior but the meaning they make of their life experiences. Adler also suggested that children construct their private logic and coping strategies as they make sense out of the following issues:

> I am . . .
>
> Other people are . . .
>
> The world is . . .
>
> Therefore . . .

As shown in the figure below, critical life events are interpreted in the private logic that is the basis for a person's coping behavior. If these coping strategies "work," or have the desired outcome, they will likely persist. Even maladaptive approaches make logical sense to the youth—providing protection, respect, or other rewards. When children continue chronic self-defeating behavior, it must be producing a payoff, even if this payoff is not obvious from their superficial behavior.

Figure 2

Why do youth persist in defiant and self-defeating behavior?

Critical life events

····▶ interpreted in private logic

····▶lead to coping behaviors

····▶that have some desired outcome

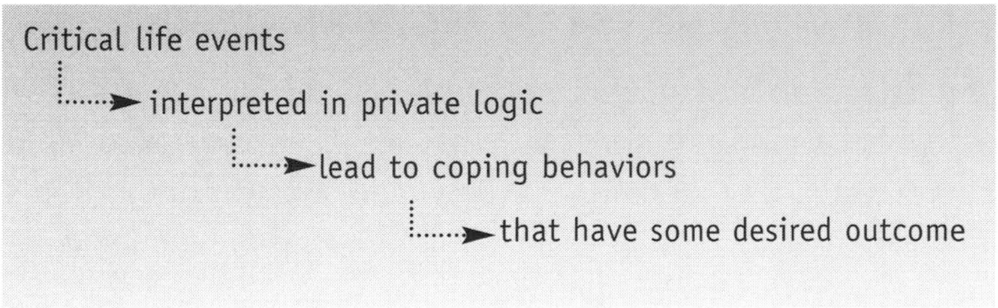

The most powerful of beliefs about self, others, and the world is whether to trust or distrust.[6] A child who has learned that adults are a source of protection will seek them out in times of crisis. But a child who has learned to distrust adults will view them as indifferent or even dangerous. Because the need for trusting relationships is so powerful, its absence is extremely unsettling and evokes powerful negative emotions such as shame, fear, and anger. Children cut off from adults often grieve and ruminate over their loss. They may sink into hopeless depression or strike out in violent rage. Instead of seeking out other caring adults, some may push everyone away to avoid human bonds. Using private logic, these are "logical" coping strategies for a distrustful child, as Melinda explains:

> My counselor was trying to pry things out of me so I told her she was a nosy b----. I once told a person a big thing, and she stabbed me in the back. I'm not making that mistake again, I'm not telling my coun- selor sh--. I won't trust anybody except myself.

The private logic of distrustful children is usually rooted in mis- treatment or traumatic events. Long after the original danger has passed, the child is still wary. Many life stories for angry, adult-wary youth follow scripts of "you don't care" and "you can't control me." Every human brain constructs beliefs about the world based on available evidence. When experiences with adults have been hostile and coercive, these experiences will shape a child's private logic and coping style. Psychologists define coping as the various ways people try to successfully meet the demands of a conflict situation.[7] Those who can only see a youth's survival strategies as "criminal thinking" are them- selves trapped in a mind-set of professional pessimism.[8]

Understanding the logic behind troubled behavior is not the same as excusing inappropriate behavior. We all choose to act in certain ways. The question is: Why would a youth keep making such bad decisions? Only when we understand private logic does seemingly senseless behavior make sense.

Jeffrey's Battle

We are indebted to Jeffrey for helping us reconstruct his trou- bled life. When we first met Jeffrey, he was sixteen and facing charges in adult court. We helped him gain admission to a residential treatment program and worked with him until he completed his high school equivalency certificate and gained independence as a young adult.

As a small child, Jeffrey lived a turbulent life, at various times shifting between his mother, father, and other male relatives. Allegations of sexual and physical abuse could not be documented, but Jeffrey's behavior suggested that he must have been abused. When he entered school, he talked of killing and being killed, showed attention problems, was impulsive, and had outbursts of temper. He set fires, ran from school, and physically assaulted children and staff. Jeff was also a curious, outgoing, and engaging child who craved affection and attention.

Jeffrey was probably abused before he had the language skills to report this abuse. We assume that he responded to the abuse with the private logic that people were treating him unfairly and he needed to act in self-defense. As a result of this private logic, discipline or punishment would cause Jeff to assume that he was under attack. Jeffrey did everything in his power to fight back. For example, in second grade, school authorities reported that Jeff was repeatedly making drawings decorated with profanity. One of these creative products, two jack-o'-lanterns labeled "sh--, dum a--, ho" in Jeffrey's childish script, remained in his case file for a decade. The principal sent a note to Jeffrey's mother that "writing notes of that sort, or using that type of language, *is not acceptable at school under any circumstances.*" The principal added that since Jeff previously had been punished for similar offenses, he now would be deprived of recess privileges for four days. Variations of this incident would be repeated over years of interventions where frustrated adults unsuccessfully tried to use consequences to control Jeff, instead of trying to understand what triggered and supported his disruptive behavior.

By third grade, Jeff was impossible to manage. A school psychologist noted that he was very closed about circumstances or problems at home or at school. One test the psychologist gave Jeff had a lie scale, and Jeff scored as answering *untruthfully* eighty percent of the time. Jeff's skill at protecting his history was reflected in his poor score on the lie scale.

Of all the documents in Jeff's case file, the one that best describes his private logic was penned by his own hand when he was ten years old. As a consequence for misbehavior, Jeff's teacher made him write an essay on how he felt about what he had done. Jeff let her have it:

> I feel fine . . . that's all I have to say. So there.
>
> And if I had my way, I would not go to schoole [sic]. So there.
>
> I do not want to write or do not have to listen to you. I do not want to. So there. And I do not care what I call anyone. So there.
>
> And I do not care about anything I do to somebody. So there.
>
> That's all I have to write so I'm not saying anything more.

When encountering a student like Jeff, most people only see the "outside kid" and fail to understand the "inside kid," to use terms shared by youth work trainer Mark Freado.[9] Jeffrey's provocative essay is an example of the outside kid. Viewing only his lack of remorse, it would be easy to conclude that this is a child without a conscience. But, when we understand the inside kid, we meet a hurting but courageous youngster defending himself against a world that has violated him.

At age twelve, Jeff was briefly hospitalized for suicidal and assaultive behavior. Reports describe him as disruptive, non-compliant, manipulative, and provocative towards peers and adults. There is no indication that any professional was able to discover what Jeffrey was really thinking about the life he had tried to end. Instead, reports ruled out brain disorders or "treatable" psychiatric illness. Jeff is described in language that says, between the lines, here comes a budding sociopath, as shown in his case record:

Jeff has a long-standing history of hurting others and showing no remorse for these actions. The quality of his interpersonal relationships indicates poor ability to form close attachments. These are problems for which there is no pharmacological intervention.

In seventh grade, a school psychologist described Jeff as manipulative, artistic, and usually cheerful with a good sense of humor. One evaluator saw Jeff as wanting meaningful relationships but afraid of getting close to people: "If Jeff would try to work through some of his trust issues in therapy, then he could learn how to identify and cope with feelings."

Jeff passed between special education programs, child psychiatric centers, and residential schools, constantly becoming better at fighting adults and getting kicked out of programs. He pierced his ears with staples and tacks, carved a gang symbol on his arm, and once even urinated in a time-out room. Peers thought his crazy defiance was cool, and he enlisted them in his attacks on adults. Eventually, psychiatric programs said Jeff was too delinquent for them, and delinquency programs viewed him as too psychiatric. Having exhausted all residential placements by age sixteen, Jeff was returned to his mother's home. Soon he was involved in a knife incident with his brother. At that point, we agreed to work with Jeff and provide school and court officials with our recommendations.

When we first met, Jeff was wearing baggy pants with a belt hanging to his knees—a general street appearance. He was cordial and we established rapport on a superficial level. We told him we had reviewed his files and found that many people had been trying to figure out why he kept getting into trouble over the years. Jeff replied that he had taken "every medication made" but none of them helped, except perhaps Ritalin for his hyperactivity. Jeff added that he doesn't trust counselors because "they treat me like I am crazy and want to mess with my head." When we said that he certainly seems to be skillful at keeping them from discovering what his problems are, he smiled.

Jeff was hypervigilant throughout our conversation, his eyes darting around and examining everything in sight. At one point he discovered the frame of my glasses was bent and demonstrated how to straighten it. Jeff tried to read our notes, so we showed them to him and asked him to correct them if we got something wrong.

He said that people say he is violent or crazy, but he likes to act that way to keep people intimidated. "I don't care what people think," he said. We suggested to Jeff that maybe he does care. After a bit of humorous verbal sparring, he said that was true, but he thought it was nobody's business how he feels. Jeff denied ever missing his father, ever crying, and so forth. His responses did not appear to be clinical denial—being out of touch with reality—but rather a very effective conversation-stopper for any counselor trying to open touchy topics.

Jeff was trying to present the image of a delinquent. He liked to dress cool and use street slang like a gang wanna-be. He loved adventure, such as hanging out of a car going fifty miles per hour, and other reckless behavior. He wore his delinquency as a badge of macho pride with tough talk about how girls like him and how he can "beat up people who mess with me." In his logic, if someone started a problem, he was entitled to finish it. Jeff's thinking was marked by blaming others, minimizing his own misdeeds, and mislabeling delinquency as an achievement. Beneath his tough shell, however, there was a soft side to Jeff. He shared that he likes to help little kids, but few see this side of him because he cannot afford to appear soft or he might be called a "wuss."

Within an hour, Jeff became increasingly warm and seemed to relish attention from adults, something that is noted occasionally in his thick case history. He showed us his "fractured finger" and his homemade tattoos, like a child wanting approval but not quite knowing how to secure it. Jeff shared his goal of going to college in spite of his rocky school performance.

As our initial interview ended, Jeff proudly announced that he had finally figured out how we got him to talk: "I see what you are doing. You compliment me so I can't get mad at you." We responded, "This just shows how clever you are and how successful you can be working with your teachers and counselors when you decide to trust them." "There you go again," he said with a smile.

We concluded that Jeffrey seems to hunger for a male role model but only has found this in older delinquent peers. He was becoming increasingly delinquent in values and thinking. Breaking from this pattern would require school success, caring adults, and prosocial peers. Otherwise, we felt Jeff would default to the values of the street. When the court became involved, the judge agreed to place Jeff in a private residential treatment school. There, he had opportunities for academic success. Positive peers and caring adults refused to give up when he showed the problems that led to dismissal from other programs. Jeff completed high school and returned to live in the community.

Fight, Flight, and Fool

Trust requires a secure belief in the good intentions of another person. But when distrust is triggered, people react with three key protective strategies: fight, flight, and fool. In the story above, Jeffrey used each of these methods. In this section, we explore the protective strategies used by youth in adversarial relationships with adults. Every parent has seen these behaviors in their own children in times of conflict, but usually a trusting relationship minimizes these tactics. When these behaviors become frequent and severe, however, trust is impossible and the relationship is contaminated. Identifying fight, flight, and fool behaviors is the first step to understanding defiant and distrustful youth.

Fight: Hurt or Be Hurt

Aggression and defiance can spring from physical threats or from frustration with any of the major needs of young people. Kids without attachment rage at rejection. Failures in achievement can lead to frustration and aggression. Deprived of autonomy, youth may engage in power struggles. Without opportunities to learn altruism, youth treat others in cruel and disrespectful ways.

Issues of race, gender, and sexual orientation can also fuel conflict. Calvin, a gay adolescent, described the feeling of being cut off from both adults and peers: "I always turn and look everywhere when I'm walking. . . . I really feel insecure. . . . You have to fight mostly every day. You have to fight to get respect."[10]

Brown and Gilligan have noted that most young girls speak out freely about feelings. By adolescence, however, this voice is muted.[11] While some girls retreat, others adopt an aggressive demeanor, as seen in the private logic of Anita, an African American girl: "We don't take no crap. We don't take no kind of b.s. from nobody! That's how we are. We don't care who you are, black girls don't take no kind of trash from nobody."[12]

Children of color are vastly overrepresented in programs for youth at risk, while professionals of color are often underrepresented. In such climates, racial misunderstanding worsens distrust, and youth become highly suspicious of adult intentions. Daniel, a fourteen-year-old African American youth in a day treatment program, shared his belief that psychiatric drugs were being administered as racist attack: "The damn fools give us drugs at school. . . . It's just another way for the crackers to get us out of the educational system. Brain damage."[13]

Unless these programs provide ways to heal racism in staff and students, an antagonism based on deep historic distrust is likely to exist, even if not openly expressed. J. C. Chambers, an African American psychologist who came from a challenging background, recalls his youth: "For some time I was enrolled in a white parochial high school in Denver. I would carry a short baseball bat in my book bag, ever vigilant lest one of the racist students were to speak the terrifying "N" word, and I would have to act to defend my dignity."[14]

Flight: Leave Me Alone

It is the natural instinct for self-preservation
which causes the child to bar the educator from
his innermost nature.

—Ellen Key[15]

Youth who decide they have no effective ways to fight adults disengage. Often they retreat into depression or become self-abusive. J. F. Masterson worked with aggressive adolescents locked in a closed psychiatric facility. No longer able to fight back, they were stripped of their defenses and became extremely depressed.[16] Normal youth rely on supportive relationships in times of stress, but a person who cannot trust others must face crisis alone. The following incident was reported by the United States Department of Justice:

> Camilla had a history of being sexually abused and became violent when placed in residential treatment. Then she was transferred by tribal authorities to a youth prison where most inmates were felons held under contract with the Federal Bureau of Prisons. While there she wrote a letter to her mother describing sexual abuse by a male guard. Some days after the alleged offense, she was interviewed by a male police officer. Camilla was vague and so authorities were quick to conclude that nothing had happened. The following day, Camilla hung herself in her cell.[17]

Suicide is the ultimate example of flight behavior. Quite obviously, it is not possible to obtain an accurate report on an alleged rape when a white, male officer interrogates a disturbed, sexually abused, American Indian girl.

Many youth find silence to be one of few tactics that gives them control over adults. Girls in particular said they would sulk and refuse to answer; they knew this silence would frustrate the adult. Said Melinda, "I wanted to make them as miserable as I was." Woody noted, "When I decide I am not talking, I just sit there, but I'm not bored. It's actually a way to outwit them. They are trying their hardest to break through and you just sit back laughing inside. It lets me know I am better than they are. Victory accomplished!"

Sometimes flight behavior is healthy. We are all inclined to retreat from threat. Sometimes treatment professionals force young people to open up buried problems when they are not yet ready. Brian Raychaba of Canada, a former youth in care, attributes much of youths' resistance to treatment to a positive desire to keep control of their own lives. Often they are forced by well-meaning adults or peer groups to confront incidents of abuse and feelings they are not yet ready to disclose. Speaking for youth in care, Brian says, "Allow us time just to be children. Forcing us to 'deal with the issues' at such an early age constitutes a theft of our childhood."[18]

Fool: Meet My Mask

"Fool me once, shame on you; fool me twice, shame on me," is the unspoken, but clearly practiced, mantra of manipulative kids. Figuring out how to deceive adults takes practice, and these children begin early. Children learn to deceive others by about age three. This is a normal adaptive human strategy, since in many situations it is important not to show one's feelings. For example, a child who is intimidated by a peer may try to appear unafraid even though that is not their honest emotion at the moment. Even preschool children can mask their internal state by changing their facial expressions or behavior. They brush crumbs from their faces and coyly smile, "No, Mommy, I wasn't in the cookie jar."

Even small children are clever at reading subtle emotional reactions in adults.[19] Children who have experienced adult brutality have more reason than most to figure out how to fool adults. They have learned to read adult emotions so they can try to avoid or appease dangerous or unpredictable adults.

As they mature, children develop increasingly sophisticated skills in deceiving others. Deception actually requires one important diagnostic skill: empathy. The child has to understand the perspective of the other individual in order to trick them.[20] Ironically, youth labeled as lacking conscience usually have considerable ability to understand what others think and feel. If they could not take the perspective of others, they would be powerless to fool them. "Manipulative" youth have well-developed tools to figure out adults; they just are not motivated to care for people they see as antagonists. Instead, these youth reserve their ability to show care and loyalty for their band of friends.

Until we asked youth in conflict to help us understand the strategies they use to outwit adults, we realized we had underestimated their skill. Jeffrey was eager to give us extensive instruction in the fine points of deceiving adults. Afterward, he proudly reported to the staff at his alternative school that "I am helping Seita and Brendtro write their book—we made a two-hour tape." Jeffrey, whose background was described earlier in this chapter, relates his strategies:

> I didn't trust any counselors, so I would study them very carefully. The first rule is to always look them in the eyes. This makes them very uncomfortable, and you can also tell if they are not telling you the truth. If I wanted them to think I was nervous, I would look down, wiggle my legs a lot so they would think I was ADD. All the while they are watching me, I check out the way they present themselves. Are they laid-back and calm, or are they trying to look good? One psychologist sat up straight for an hour. It can't possibly feel good to do that, so I know he was just trying to look good.
>
> Sometimes I flooded them with pieces of confusing information. I described myself as if I have two different personalities, but later drop information that makes it seem I am just pretending to have a split personality. Now they have no way to explain

Figure 3

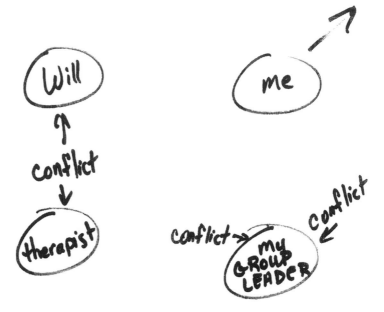

Jeffrey drew this diagram to compare his approach of outwitting adults to that used by Will in the movie *Good Will Hunting*. Will provoked conflict with his therapist. Jeffrey prefers to create the conflict inside the therapist's mind. Knowing professionals don't want to give up on difficult kids, Jeffrey tries to make it appear that nothing will work to reach him. Once the conflict is inside of the adult, Jeffrey says, "I can smile and walk away."

things. I mess up the minds of my counselors, and they are in conflict.

I watched *Good Will Hunting* and saw that Will kept trying to attack his therapist, Sean. I enjoyed that, but I use a different system. Let me show you with these drawings. [Jeffrey drew two circles representing Sean and Will and then connected them with an arrow marked "conflict." Then he drew two other circles showing himself and a therapist, but he explained that he wanted the conflict to be entirely in the therapist's mind, not between him and the therapist.] I know their job is to keep trying to succeed with difficult kids, so I use this information to put them into conflict with themselves. They want to succeed but I make it seem that there is no possible way that they can. Whatever they try, nothing works. They were trying to mess with me, and now I've messed with them. The conflict is inside of them.

Vulnerable people construct a false front. For example, youth with deep conflicts often project an image that they have no problems. Scott was such an I-couldn't-care-less youth. Underneath his false front, however, he cared very deeply. He worried endlessly about whether his adoptive parents really loved him or if they wanted to be rid of him. To test their loyalty, he would say, "You aren't even my parents." He would spend weeks living with families of peers wondering why his parents didn't make him come home. He really wanted to reconcile but feared rejection. He even thought about searching for his biological parents but decided it was hard enough to get along with the parents he had. He adds "but I do think they should pass a law so parents who adopt out children would have to put their DNA on file and, when we get to be 18, we could get this to test our genetics." This highly introspective youth was called "shallow" in some case records.

A principal reason many youth hide problems is to prevent future hurt. They use various strategies to shroud their painful inner life. Mary's father was arrested for impregnating her sister. He went to prison, and her sister went to foster care. "During the next year, my mother's boyfriend raped me, but I told no one. I was too frightened of being taken away." Terry also carefully guarded his private logic: "They think they have me figured out. There is no way in hell I am going to let anybody figure me out." Jeffrey perhaps best captures the motivation of adult-wary youth to outwit adults: "I had to be a better psychologist than the psychologists. They are doing it to make a living; I'm doing it for life."

Mind Games: Youth as Folk Psychologists

Disturbed children are often skillful at detecting and exploiting the weaknesses of adults. Indeed this is one reason that adults reject them and call them disturbed.

—Nicholas Hobbs[21]

Nicholas Hobbs was president of the American Psychological Association and a pioneer in developing re-education programs for troubled children. In his book, *The Troubled and Troubling Child*, he described such youth as *folk psychologists*. Many have developed remarkable abilities at "diagnosing and managing" adults. They become expert folk psychologists in the same way a person masters any challenging task: repeated practice and experience.

In the acquisition of complex skills, such as playing chess or piloting a plane, the difference between a novice and a master is *pattern recognition*. A novice chess player can only visualize one move at a time, but a master has "seen it all" and can anticipate many moves ahead, even to the point of winning against a computer. Similarly, a new pilot is preoccupied with trying to keep track of the half dozen instruments used to monitor basic flight. But a seasoned pilot with thousands of hours of flight time can quickly detect subtle patterns in hundreds of indicators and make the necessary changes. Likewise, kids with years of experience battling adults become skilled at evasion and reading adult behavior. Drawing on thousands of hours of "fight time," they have uncanny abilities to find the weakness of their adversaries.

The ability of youth to detect the Achilles' heel of adults was cleverly portrayed in the movie *Good Will Hunting*. Upon first meeting his therapist, Sean, young Will began testing to discover how he might provoke this latest enemy. Will experimented with various insults until he discovered that Sean was touchy about his deceased wife and he finally got Sean to lose his temper.

A real-world example of the ability of youth to find adult weaknesses is seen in this account of Reggie, a student at a camp for disturbed boys. At the end of his first day at the University of Michigan Fresh Air Camp, Reggie had alienated all the counselors in his cabin. Upon first meeting a counselor who had a mole on his cheek, he said, "Wouldn't it be better if you had a doctor cut off that brown spot so people don't have to look at it?" To another he volunteered, "My auntie was plump like you, but she went on a special diet and now she looks great. Would you like me to find out about the diet?" He made equally "helpful" comments about a counselor with ugly glasses and another who was poorly coordinated. Another member of the team had no apparent physical flaws, but he told her, "You know it's strange. When I look at your face—and then when I listen to your voice—well, the two of them just don't go together."

Our most challenging youth are skilled at diagnosing adults while masking their own intentions. Unless such young people form partnerships with adults, they use their abilities to keep adults from understanding them or having influence in their lives. As one youth told us, "Adults are trying to mess with my mind, so I will mess with theirs." The major strategies used by kids to play mind games with adults are conceal and confuse, connect and corrupt, and sabotage.

Conceal and Confuse

To gain an advantage over an enemy, many youth hide their real intentions and send out false signals. Just as the spies in the Central Intelligence Agency (CIA) use disguises and disinformation, so do distrustful youth. Roni was an expert at using misinformation to confuse others and conceal her real nature. Life on the street and in shelters had taught her to be guarded. When she was finishing high school and turning her life around, she shared with us her strategy of deception:

> The first rule was to never let them know anything. I would put up a front and say the opposite of the truth. I would sit relaxed, making eye contact. I would tell them there were no problems or that

things were getting better. I tried to make them feel they were helping, so I told about some trivial problems that I didn't mind talking about. Or I might boast about things that I hadn't even done to create a false impression. Life is a stage but you have to remember your lines or your stories won't jibe.

When staff started asking me questions, I asked them stuff about their life. I could care less, but it got them off of me. "Do you have kids? … What is your husband like? Isn't it terrible what some people are doing to mess up their lives with drugs?" All of this chatter created the impression that I was opening up so they wouldn't try to figure me out so much.

Why was I afraid? I saw them as a threat. They would use what I told them against me in reports, and the courts or others would find out. I also thought they didn't have a right to know. They did not care; it was only their job. They only would have a right to know if there was a good relationship between us. Some did try, but my first reaction was they would not stick around long or maybe they would give up on me and I would get hurt. I got kicked out of a lot of places where people didn't care if I went to the street.

When they made me see psychologists, I denied anything was wrong with me, it was everybody else. Saying I had no problems didn't work because they said I was just putting up a front. So I had to go to level two: "Ok, I do have a front, but that's all. I don't even notice it; it is so natural. How am I supposed to change?" The trick was to make them think I wanted their help. When I turned the problem back to them, "How do I stop putting up a front?" they were stumped. Nobody thought to ask me why I was putting up a front.

I didn't want to talk, but if I totally refused, this would work against me. So I told them trivia and half-truths. One person asked me if I had ever thought about dying. I knew she was trying to find out if I was depressed or suicidal so I turned the question around and asked if she had ever thought of death. This shocked her, and then she said, "We're here to work on your problems."

You have to be very attentive and watch how the counselor is reacting. If they are engrossed, you have their attention. If they are looking around, they are trying to figure out how to trick you. If they are cross-checking your story, they are trying to trip you up. If they were getting too close, I would stop them by concocting a huge problem like being raped or seeing somebody die. I wanted them to think, "She started to open up today." But I knew I couldn't just talk my way out of trouble; I had to show changes in behavior. I usually timed improvements just before my court hearings.

Roni hopes to go to college and prepare for a career in youth work. She is already doing volunteer work with younger at-risk girls. We noticed how they look up to her. They seem to sense she understands. She has been in their place.

Connect and Corrupt

Sometimes, corruption of an adult begins with a positive bond and the youth pushing limits to see how far they might go. A potent tactic used by some youths is to actually build connections with a certain staff member in order to use them for other purposes. Such a youth will go to considerable effort to form a relationship in order to exploit the adult in some way.

Youth who become comfortable with an adult commonly try to overlook some rule. Paul, a youth in an Australian detention center, had begun to build a good relationship with his counselor, Harry, when he started to test the limits. "I know you smoke and so do I. Harry, I know you can't give me smokes, but now that we're mates, maybe you could just store some cigarettes in the couch, and I could borrow some when I am here. Nobody would know." Harry responded appropriately, "We both would know."

Staff who become involved in activities that compromise their integrity are setting out on a pathway that can lead to major problems. One example is when an adult acts as if he or she is a peer of a youth. Dusty, a student in an alternative school, describes such a case:

> I try to get real close to staff, get them to talk about their personal life. It makes it harder for them to control me. I had this staff person Ralph and I could see he was not happy with his job. I saw little clues that he wasn't getting along with administration or other staff. I took this as a chance to encourage him to tell me about how he hated his job and was looking for other employment. "I don't blame you, this place sucks," I told Ralph. Soon he let me slide on rules. But other staff noticed and confronted him. Then he switched to a "tough guy" role, and I stood up to him. He got so mad that he hit me and was fired for this. Maybe I should have felt bad, but then, it's obvious that Ralph didn't really belong in this work.

The blurring of the boundaries between adult and youth reaches its extreme when helping relationships become sexual encounters. Fourteen-year-old Kristi had been abandoned as a small child by her mother and for years moved from one foster home to another. Finally, after she threatened to kill a female teacher, she was sent to a day treatment center. She had terrible relationships with female staff but was very seductive with males. She attached herself to one of the teacher-aides, a family man twice her age. One day on a school field trip to an amusement park, both of them sneaked off together to the staff member's apartment. This offense would not have been discovered except that Kristi bragged to her friends about having sex with the man. When investigated, she denied anything happened but the man was charged as a sexual offender.

One should not infer that these youths do not want genuine relationships with adults; however, these kids know the power of relationships and want to use their relationships with adults for their own power agenda. Often they are practicing coping strategies of connect and corrupt that others have used on them. In the example of Kristi above, staff later learned that she had previously had other relationships with adult pedophiles. While it may seem safest for staff to avoid such youths, these kids desperately need to experience relationships without exploitation.

Sabotage Adults

Youth who distrust adults are more likely to turn to peers for support and advice. Jerry, who was in a substance abuse treatment program, remarked:

> People your own age are going through the same
> stuff, and you can connect with them. Somebody
> older telling you what to do, you just block him out.
> You don't want to listen to them, because they are
> older and they think they have power over you.

Youth are also inclined to help peers in trouble. Dan has had many problems in school for "mouthing off." When a girl dropped her books and papers all over the hall and other kids laughed, he helped her pick them up. "I like being nice to people who are picked on by others." Peer support also extends to joining forces with other kids who are in confrontations with adult authority figures. A universal problem in most schools and youth programs is that youth bond together in defiance of adults. Angry kids get in individual contests with adults, but a group of them makes for a tournament. As discussed in Chapter One, negative peer groups are powerful reinforcers for rebellious and antisocial behavior. In an ideal world, delinquents would never be put together because they cheer one another on in a carnival of outrageous behavior. But keeping troubled kids separate is unworkable in many alternative schools or treatment settings populated with swarms of sassy kids. Such places become spawning grounds for delinquent subcultures. In negative climates, youth harass and victimize one another and gang up against adults. We have written extensively about how to build positive peer cultures.[22] Here we look briefly at the challenge presented by negative group cultures.

The skill with which youth can sabotage adult programs is shown in the following observations of a group of early adolescents in a treatment program for sexually acting-out boys. Most had been sexually abused in childhood and subsequently became abusers of younger children, typically siblings or other children in their foster homes. When we began, the group leader, Dr. E., was trying to welcome a new boy, twelve-year-old Joel, to the group. As soon as he entered the room, Joel loudly protested, "I don't belong in a sexual offenders group because I am not a sexual offender; I just have serious behavior problems!" Several boys quickly accused Joel of being in denial, and he bristled. Dr. E. restored order by asking the boys to give examples of recent situations that had triggered sexual fantasies to show Joel how the group operates.

Adam came forth with an entertaining story of seeing a bosom, which was a trigger. Dr. E. asked him to provide more specific detail including what he thought and felt. Adam initially went into a period of silliness where he said the bosom was "yummy" and made him feel happy and his behavior was to want to fondle the "squishy bosom." All the boys were greatly entertained, but Dr. E. reminded them of the seriousness of the group, prompting Adam to be even more specific. On a field trip to a nearby town, Adam had seen a beautiful girl who reminded him of Miss Vanna Humpalot, a character in an Austin Powers movie. Adam provided an entertainment-quality impersonation of Austin Powers with quotations from the movie, such as "You make me horny, baby!" He reported his fantasy was to "hump" girls. The therapist made him use the proper term: sexual intercourse. Later, Dr. E. said that he knew they were making a mockery of treatment, but he had never seen an Austin Powers movie and could not follow the humor.

Dr. E. then called on Nathan, reminding him he had been in the group the longest and should be a good example for the new member. Nathan agreed and reported a recent incident in which viewing the rear of a cow was a trigger that made him think of sex. He then stood up and convincingly demonstrated how the cow sashayed with its rear. "The bull was standing by, not mounting the cow, but his thing was hanging from his stomach." After prompting by Dr. E., Nathan used the correct word for the "thing," responding with "the penis was hanging from the stomach." Nathan reported his fantasy: he wished he were a bull and could "do it" with any females at any time he wanted. The group got into a rowdy discussion of whether this was a bad fantasy or not.

By now, Joel was getting quite interested and no longer feeling threatened by group therapy. He was discovering this was just another way to hassle staff, an activity at which he excelled. Throughout the meeting, different group members would shout out rowdy comments. All the while, Dr. E. unsuccessfully tried the techniques of ignoring, warning in a stern voice, and issuing one-dollar fines for lack of seriousness. The boys would stop momentarily but then return to taunting. The low point of the meeting came when the group debated in veiled terms the possible color of the therapist's penis.

Other, more reserved youths took turns telling less humorous but no more serious stories. After all the other boys had reported, Dr. E. asked Joel if he was ready to make a contribution. Joel repeated that he wasn't a sexual offender but offered to share an incident where "I was very, very naughty." Joel took the stage with an account of a time his mother ran over his skateboard with her car. This had been the trigger. His thoughts and feelings were "she made me pissed, and I was going to run over her car with my skateboard." Roars of laughter came from the group. Joel continued, "Later that night, I took the keys and ran my mother's car into the pond, and I didn't feel guilty. I felt good." The group leader thanked Joel for sharing, and Joel appeared pleased.

Immediately after the meeting, Joel came up to us and said, "It never happened. They wanted me to tell a story so I just made one up." After only one peer group meeting, Joel had figured out how to manipulate the system. Of course, Joel is something of a professional at manipulation, having lived on the streets several years. In his words, "I've been kicked out of forty places and I am going to get kicked out of this place, too."

Battle Plans

Highly distrustful youth use clever tactics to attack, evade, or outmaneuver adults who try to control or connect with them. Some youth plan their actions like battle tacticians, while others react without apparent forethought, reflexively engaging in defensive behavior. Whether conscious coping or unconscious defense, the intent is self-protection.

Many youth who appear to act impulsively and without thinking are actually drawing on defensive responses set in habitual memory. Human brains can detect hostility or rejection in less than a quarter of a second; before a person is consciously aware of these cues, emotions and behavior are triggered.[23] For example, a youth who was abused as a child may lash out at the slightest provocation. To an observer, what appears to be an impulsive act may well be a fast draw by a kid reared on the mean streets.

Given the sophistication of troubled youth, Nicholas Hobbs concluded that adults who work with these individuals need stable personalities and solid interpersonal skills. Most of this is learned in a lifetime of unique experience, which makes each of us a folk psychologist. Hobbs suggested that in developing effective staff "selection is more powerful than training." As Hobbs concludes, if a young person does not succeed in reeducation, this was probably not a failure of the child, but a limitation of the adult's skill and strategy.[24]

Rules of Engagement

Young people can become very skilled at figuring out and outwitting the adults in their lives. Drawing on private logic honed by years of conflict, they employ strategies to diagnose, attack, avoid, and deceive adults. Only as we understand their private logic and decode the purpose of their behavior are we able to

avoid reactively adversarial relationships. Some common coping
strategies used by youth in conflict with adults:

Outmaneuvering Adults

Gathering Intelligence: Checking out the enemy.

- Hypervigilance. *This situation is dangerous.*
- Assuming the worst. *You're just like all the rest.*
- Testing. *Let's find out what will happen.*
- Detection. *Now I see how you operate.*
- Targeting. *I've found your weak spot.*

Fight: Hurt or be hurt.

- Blaming. *It's all your fault.*
- Hard shell. *You don't scare me.*
- Strategic anger. *I can intimidate you.*
- Overpower. *You can't control me.*
- Profanity and insults. *Your mother . . .*
- Divide and conquer. *I'll split the adults.*
- Enlisting fellow warriors. *It's us against them.*
- Physical abuse. *I'm a dangerous person.*

Flight: Leave me alone.

- Emotional distance. *Don't let anyone get close.*
- Silence. *You can't make me talk.*
- Playing dumb. *Whatever.*
- Withdrawal. *I'll crawl into my shell.*
- Self-medicating. *I'll get stoned.*
- Zero tolerance. *Kick me out.*
- Flee. *I am outta here.*
- Giving up. *Why should I keep on living?*

Fool: Meet my mask.

- Smile them away. *Nothing bothers me.*
- Flatter them. *You really understand kids like me.*
- Tell them what they want to hear. *You're so right.*
- Diversion. *Keep them from the real problems.*
- Act weird. *I'm a psycho.*
- Defuse their power. *Punish me—see if I care.*
- Get them to disclose. *I know your secrets.*
- Seduction. *I've got you just where I want you.*

As will be seen in the following chapter, many adults reciprocate this adversarial fight, flight, and fool stance.

Endnotes

[1] Rapaport 1960.

[2] Braithwaite 1989.

[3] Guarino-Ghezzi, Godfrey, and Bankowski 1997, 182.

[4] Bandura 1986.

[5] Adler 1930, 153.

[6] Erikson 1950.

[7] Zeidner and Endler 1995.

[8] Jacobs 1995.

[9] Freado 2001.

[10] DuBeau 1997, 24.

[11] Brown and Gilligan 1992.

[12] Taylor, Gilligan, and Sullivan 1996, 72.

[13] Way 1993, 4.

[14] Chambers 2000, 14.

[15] Key 1909.

[16] Masterson 1985.

[17] U.S. Department of Justice 2000.

[18] Raychaba 1992, 6.

[19] Lewis 1997.

[20] Ibid.

[21] Hobbs 1994, 108–109.

[22] Vorrath and Brendtro 1985.

[23] Research by Robert Zajonc and colleagues at the University of Michigan has shown that everything we see, hear, touch, or smell triggers automatic and unconscious associations within 200 milliseconds. In that instant, the brain has already evaluated this input to decide whether the situation is positive or threatening. See Azar 1998.

[24] Hobbs 1994.

Antagonistic Encounters

He's a good kid! And I won't see this happen to him! I won't see you make him feel like a failure, too!

—Sean Maguire, Will Hunting's therapist, *Good Will Hunting*

Everything had gone wrong, and I knew something bad would happen again soon. I wasn't disappointed. Just when I started to make friends with the other outcasts at the Receiving Home, they sent me away.

For years I was shuttled around among sometimes-abusive foster homes, soulless group homes, and impersonal orphanages and detention centers. Each failed placement tore away more of my soul. I was sick of being shifted here and there among people I didn't trust. Why should I live with strangers? Why couldn't I be with my mom? Why was I even born? Each new home, neighborhood, and school was different. It was like moving into a foreign country where I couldn't speak the language. Nobody tried to speak mine.

At first some of the foster families seemed nice enough. I would put my best face on and say and do the right things. I had become a pretty good actor, but I couldn't maintain this facade for long. I hated living in fake families. Soon our fronts—mine and theirs—crumbled, and the outcome fed my feelings of rejection.

I blew all of my foster care placements intentionally, each and every one. I wanted all of my foster parents to think that I was "crazy," unmanageable, and not at all interested in being part of a family or in being loved. In my mind, all adults had betrayed me, so I must be worthless.

Adults were my enemies, and I wanted to get them mad so I could hate them even more. If adults tried to bribe me with a gift, I would destroy it right in front of them. If they tried to correct me, I would curse and scream at the top of my lungs. I knocked over lamps and tables. Once I was forced to eat a bar of soap for swearing; the stinging pain made me gag, but I refused to apologize. I tried to ruin food by putting salt in the sugar bowl; they spanked me and sent me to bed without supper. Once I had to pull down my pants and sit nude on the sharp rim of a #10 can. I pretended it didn't hurt.

Sometimes, I ran away before they could send me away. I stole food to survive, and I kept adults at bay. I earned both a small victory and a large defeat as I drove away adults. Since I felt powerless, this small victory gave me control over where and with whom I would not live. My large defeat was making a purposeful decision to refuse love.

Between foster homes, I would ricochet back to the Receiving Home. It always took them some time to talk another unsuspecting foster family into giving me a try. At least in the Receiving Home, there were other kids like me, and having given up on adults, we found one another. "Hey, John is back!" some Receiving Home boy would holler.

My friend Sammy and I would run away constantly. When Winfield and Ron joined us on our runaways, we became a multicultural family. Our mutual bond was abandonment by our families. As the oldest, Sammy became commander of our little crew. Our code was to stick together through everything, and we did. It did not matter that what we were doing might be illegal or that we might hurt others or ourselves. What counted was that we belonged. In this small group, I developed power that I never had in the larger adult world. By joining together in our little gang, we could make others fear us.

We would steal from stores. One night, we were hanging around outside of a liquor store and had hatched a plan to mug some unsuspecting customer who might be coming out with booze or money. We targeted an elderly couple. They must have become suspicious, because they sneaked out the back door.

I was on a crusade to behave badly enough that only my mother would take me back. I had lots of feelings inside, but on the surface, I was getting harder and colder. My pathway toward delinquency was documented in my case file: "John seems to put his faith in various kinds of power (e.g., money, strength, etc.) rather than people, and he has adopted a kind of philosophy of grab what you need and the hell with anyone else."

All of my failed relationships with adults made me believe that I was shamefully different. My pitiful self-concept was rooted in feelings that I was "damaged goods." My mother and the man I had called father had abandoned me. The system had done little to reclaim me. Acceptance, protection, and love were not forthcoming. My documented self-worth was zero: "Part of John's anger is directed toward himself. John expresses the idea that he is somehow at fault—that he is 'bad' and therefore deserves the rejection that he has received. He views himself in very derogatory terms (a rat, a mean monster, a dirty pig, etc.) and now assumes that no one will accept him or care for him."

At that point, I rejected most overtures by adults, unless I needed counsel in time of crisis. Then I briefly used adults to weather the storm, only to push them away again once it was over by being aloof, cold, and distant. If that did not work, I distanced myself with a verbal barrage of insults and swearing. My barbed words and nonverbal messages said, "I am pissed off at the world and ready to fight about it." By keeping my distance from adults, I developed a safe space or comfort zone.

Of course, adults didn't have a clue about what was going on in my mind, since my behavior camouflaged my true feelings and needs. I rejected all their efforts to connect with me even though that was what I desperately wanted. My strategy of accepting people temporarily and then suddenly rejecting them caused adults to be unwilling to risk being hurt by me. I had protected myself right into relationship hell. Even the professionals who were supposed to help were giving up hope:

> *It is now apparent that John cannot form a parent-child relationship within any foster home. By the same token, I would judge that his placement in a residential treatment agency would not be the answer to this boy's problems. This would only support his withdrawal tendencies, sharpen his resentment and anger, and intensify his fantasies of someday returning to his mother. Perhaps a better solution would be to keep John in a foster home and forewarn the foster parents that they should not try to form a parent-child relationship.*

In the long run, my survival strategy of rejecting love was no survival strategy at all. My life was empty and meaningless. I had been a resounding success at making myself unlovable. Did anyone even care if I lived or died? At night when all alone, I thought about how I might kill myself. But then I remembered that my mother had taught me that life is eternal. Even killing myself would not let me escape. My pain would last forever.

The Pessimism Lens

Einstein noted that two perceivers in separate locations are likely to experience the same event differently.[1] Management and personal development consultant Stephen R. Covey agrees that we each use a private lens to view the world and decide how to act.[2]

Few of us actually decide to see the world through a positive or negative lens. Instead, we operate from a lifetime of different personal, cultural, and educational experiences. Sometimes past events or even our professional training interfere with understanding the real world in which young people live.

Viewing a youth through a *Pessimism Lens* magnifies failures and flaws and encourages punishment or "flaw-fixing." With an *Opportunity Lens*, the focus shifts to potentials, and the goal switches to enlisting the young person as a partner in his or her own healing.

We call kids "disruptive" or "violent" because their behavior disrupts or violates us. As an outsider, we may think we are viewing a problem with detached objectivity when actually we are using a mindset of blame. By knowing what a young person thinks and feels—their private logic—we get a different view of the problem based on perspective-taking and empathy. The most accurate view of a situation requires many sources of information.

Unfortunately, in current public debates about youth violence, pessimism clouds out all other viewpoints. We are deluged by angry youth-bashing rhetoric from every quarter. The media, politicians, and public all have different ideas about what to do with the "worst of the worst."[3] Youth professionals can also be pessimistic, depending on whether they see youth through the Opportunity Lens or the Pessimism Lens. They either search for the criminal or the hero within the young person.[4]

Youth react negatively to adults who view them through the Pessimism Lens. Even the most troubled young person wants to be healthy and normal. To a child trying to preserve a fragile sense of self-worth, admitting to problems is the same as being sick or crazy. The denial of problems can actually be a desire for mental health—a good sign, really.

The most destructive effect of the Pessimism Lens is that it leads to interventions based on attack, avoidance, or manipulation—also known as fight, flight, and fool. Of course, these are the same response styles used by distrustful youth. In this chapter, we identify the popular but misguided strategies of the Pessimism Lens that lead to hostility between youth and adults.

Fight: Conflict Cycles

Will [Commenting on a painting by Sean]: This is a real piece of shit.

Sean: Tell me what you really think.

Will: I think you're one step from cutting your ear off . . . .

Sean: Maybe you should be a patient and sit down.

Will: Maybe you married the wrong woman.

Sean: Maybe you should watch your mouth.

Will: That's it, isn't it? You married the wrong woman. She leave you? Was she banging someone else? . . .

[In a flash Sean has Will by the throat. Will is helpless.]

Sean: If you ever disrespect my wife again, I will end you.

—*Good Will Hunting*

Kids like Will Hunting infuriate adults. Using strategic antagonism, they can transform kind adults into brutes. Nicholas Long and colleagues describe the *conflict cycle* that can suck even well-intentioned people into power struggles and punitive reactions:

- *Stress* evokes negative thoughts, such as "everyone is against me."

- This private logic triggers negative *Feelings* such as anger or fear.

- These feelings drive *Behavior* such as aggression or avoidance.

- The youth's behavior provokes *Reactions* from others.

- These responses mirror the youth's feelings and further increase *Stress*.

What starts as a small incident escalates via a series of conflict cycles into a major crisis. Long's research on one hundred incidents of violence in New York City schools showed that most started as minor problems but grew into major aggression.[5]

Figure 4
_____

Adapted and reproduced with permission of Life Space Crisis Intervention Institute.

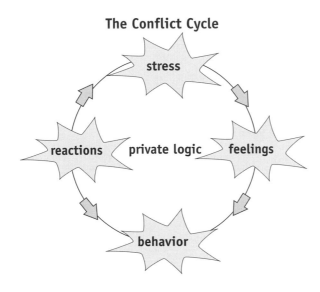

The Conflict Cycle

stress

reactions private logic feelings

behavior

_____

Conflict cycles are at the root of many ruptures in relationships between youth and adults. Adults who are locked in conflict cycles with youth are in a risky double bind. While flight and fight are normal reactions in conflict situations, both are counterproductive in working with youth. Adults who react with the fight response mirror the youth's hostility and unwittingly display aggression. If adults use flight behavior, they avoid interactions or submit to the desires of the youth, which also teaches the youth that aggression pays off.[6]

Young people who believe that they have been betrayed by the adults entrusted with their care are often thin-skinned and very sensitive to any form of hostility. They misinterpret the intent of others and return the rejection they see. Even the slightest insult can cycle into a major crisis. Too often, unaware adults feed into these conflict cycles.

Such was the case with Theo, a biracial boy raised in a hotbed of disrespect. Abused from early childhood, he entered school swinging—literally. In his private logic, others had always messed with him, and he was going to fight back. In his all-white school, Theo was teased by peers about his skin color. Recalling first grade, he said, "I told the teacher to make the kids quit making fun of me and calling me niggerish." In middle school, Theo was small for his age and kept a weapon in his book bag in case he was "dissed" by other kids. This report from his school files is a classic example of a minor conflict spiraling into major crisis as Theo provoked a male teacher into ever-intensifying conflict cycles:

> I confronted Theo and asked him why he wasn't participating in his group and why he wasn't doing the assigned activity. He responded that his group didn't want him to. I said that wasn't true and it didn't matter if they did or not, he should participate.

> Later, Theo stood up and confronted another student by saying, "Are you going to make me?" I stepped in and said, "Yes, I am going to make you sit down." I told him that he wasn't going to start anything in my class. He said he'd do anything he pleased; he didn't need us or this class. Theo got angrier and angrier while I tried to get him to sit down.

> Theo then erupted and told me, "F--- you!" I then grabbed him to sit him down. He in turn pushed me and put his fists up and wanted to fight. He said, "No one f---in' touches me," and started calling me out to fight. He said he would kick my a-- and wanted to go. I told him to get into my office. He kept refusing and swearing at me and asking me to fight.

Beginning to get very upset, I grabbed for him to push him into my office. He again pushed me away and said not to touch him and continued to try to get me to fight. He slowly made his way into my office where I told him to sit down. Theo continued to yell and swear at me and kept trying to get me to fight. At this time, he said he was going to get a gun and shoot me! He promised that he would get me somehow, some way.

Finally, he sat down. I called Mr. S. to come and take him away. Theo was still yelling and swearing at me while I was on the phone. When Mr. S. arrived, I told him the story, and I also told him I didn't want Theo back in my class. At this time, Mr. S. took Theo and left. From the time Theo said, "F--- you!" until Mr. S. arrived in my class, he continued to yell at me, swear extensively (especially f---), and ask me to fight because he was going to kick my a--.[7]

This teacher's awkward attempt to defuse a peer conflict only made him the target of Theo's anger. In Theo's private logic, the teacher became the enemy. Once the hostility started, each party in the conflict fueled the fury of the other. In a few brief minutes, Theo was transformed from one who felt victimized to one who threatened violence to others. As Nicholas Long has shown, in a conflict cycle, the adult must become a thermostat (setting the temperature) instead of a thermometer (responding to the temperature). But this teacher was unable to cool down his own emotional reactions to Theo's misbehavior. In nearly every part of this interaction, the teacher fueled Theo's fire. A review of this incident shows points in every paragraph of the teacher's report where there was a missed opportunity to de-escalate Theo's behavior. For example:

1. When peers rejected Theo, the teacher brushed this off as irrelevant. Instead, he might have tried to get peers to welcome Theo into the group.

2. When Theo was battling peers, the teacher jumped in and challenged him with "I am going to make you sit down." He wasted his role as an arbiter of conflict and became an adversary.

3. When Theo swore, the teacher reports "I then grabbed him to sit him down." The teacher directly escalated a verbal encounter to a physical contest.

4. By his own report, the teacher acknowledges that he was "beginning to get very upset." What was needed now was some distance between them. Instead, the teacher grabbed and tried to move Theo into his office, which caused Theo to make verbal threats to shoot the teacher.

5. When handing over Theo to the principal, the teacher announces he doesn't want Theo back in his class. The rejection is final.

Control Contests

Fearful of being unable to manage defiant youngsters, adults often end up creating a climate of intimidation. In many homes and schools, the goal of adults is control while the goal of youth is to avoid being controlled. Power struggles are common in many families and become particularly tense with tough kids. A national study of programs for children with behavioral and emotional problems found that most were based on "a curriculum of control" where adults who should be mentors are drawn into hostile struggles for obedience.[8] Archbishop Desmond Tutu has noted that "intimidation is merely acknowledging the weakness of your point of view."[9] Similarly many "get tough" practices with challenging kids mask adult weakness or lack of training.

Many schools and institutions rely heavily on coercive methods to manage troubled and troubling youth. The general public seems to tolerate these abuses in the false belief that brutality is necessary with the "worst of the worst." In reality, these youth are the "neediest of the needy." Adults who want to help these youth are often saddled with mean-spirited policies. An inner city Detroit teacher told us she wasn't renewing her contract because "I love the kids, but I can't deal with the system." A counselor in a youth corrections facility said: "I am quitting after twenty years. When all the directives coming down are about more security and sanctions, then even staff who are liked by the kids become suspect."

We have seen evidence that compassion is becoming *passé* even in supposedly sophisticated education and treatment programs. Demands for accountability have turned workers into scribes who spend more time cranking out reports than listening to lonely kids. A colleague suggested, perhaps we should tuck children into file cabinets so they would get more attention. At the conclusion of Life Space Crisis Intervention training, one participant remarked, "This was all very interesting, but who has time to talk with kids?"

Adults who don't listen to the "inside kid" have little empathy for their problems. When politicians in Canada were railing against prostitution by street youth, arrangements were made for young girls in the sex trade to tell them the stories of their abusive lives. As a result, calls for punishment turned into a search for positive supports. In another instance, we know of a school board member who was known for being "tough on those punks who don't want to learn." His support of expulsion was legendary until his own grandson called in a bomb threat to the school as a prank. Suddenly Granddad was bargaining for leniency for his grandson. After all, this was "a good kid who simply showed poor judgment; we should give him a second chance."

In recent years, schools and communities have encountered a group of students who have shown disruptive and self-defeating behavior for many years. Such youth suck adults into escalating power struggles, and many seem immune to traditional methods of punishment. Defying adults is cool and gives status. Kids may even laugh at punishment to impress peers or flaunt their immunity from adult authority. As one youth said: "I wear handcuffs like a showboat so that all my friends can see that I am hard. When they march me to court shackled like that, it backs up my street image."

In arriving at a solution to this problem, the answers we get depend on the questions we ask. For example, what would be the different effects of the following questions about a student with chronic behavior problems?

> What negative consequences will make this student stop this oppositional and defiant behavior?

> Why does this student continue oppositional and defiant behavior in spite of negative consequences?

The first question inevitably leads to *administering consequences* by punishing. Adults often expend great effort trying to control behavior without any knowledge of what might be maintaining the behavior. The typical solution: administer bigger doses of what hasn't worked. As the founder of behavior modification, B. F. Skinner once noted that punishment is not a teaching intervention but a sign of educational failure.[10]

The second question leads to *teaching consequences* through a problem-solving approach. The adult seeks to understand the function or purpose of the youth's behavior. Of course, just asking youth why they break rules assumes that they know and will tell. Adults need sophisticated strategies to understand the behavior and help youth disengage from entrenched patterns of conflict.

The Powerlessness of Punishment

Even severe punishment fails to deter certain strong-willed youth. For example, our colleague Michael Montgomery describes the impotence of methods once used by the Irish Republican Army (IRA) to deter joyriders or car thieves in West Belfast. The offenders were taken to the country and "kneecapped" with bullets shot into their joints. As soon as the youth were able to hobble on crutches or in plaster casts, however, they would steal another car.[11] Likewise, even Hitler's feared SS was unable to stop youth gangs who constantly defied their Nazi intimidators. The Edelweiss Pirates would maraud and then proudly sing their songs of defiance. If the IRA and Nazis couldn't control behavior with punishment, who can?

With rebellious youth, punishment serves as defiance training and fuels angry pride, giving the young people more motivation and skill for resistance. In response, the youths' defiance trains adults to become more aggressive. Nowhere is this cycle more obvious than in correctional settings. When staffed by untrained workers, such programs almost always deteriorate into gulags of abuse. This cycle was demonstrated by Marcus, whose case was transferred to open court where all confidentiality was waived. His story shows the explosive combination of vengeful adults and problem kids.

Marcus: The Road to Riot

Marcus is a tall, friendly, good-looking, fifteen-year-old, Native American youth with a family background of alcoholism and abuse. At age eight, Marcus started huffing glue and threatening to kill himself. Unknown to his mother, this was also when he was sexually abused by a neighborhood pedophile. Marcus became aggressive and clashed with his teachers, so his mother kept moving him to new schools.

When Marcus was ten, his mother finally took him to a psychologist. Marcus always kept his counseling appointments, even when it was raining, snowing, or his mother was not at home. The psychologist was beginning to understand Marcus's sexual abuse issues when she became pregnant and resigned. Marcus refused to see another counselor.

Marcus never knew his father but was attached to his stepfather, whom he called Dad. When Marcus was thirteen, his dad was brutally murdered, and Marcus told us he felt responsible for not being there to help.

Marcus soon was beyond the control of his mother as he ran the streets with violent, older, gang-involved youth. Gang conflicts spread into his middle school, and Marcus pulled a knife on a youth who had earlier threatened him with a gun.

Marcus was placed in a highly secure youth prison because an arbitrary classification scheme dictated this security level due to the knife incident. The rules were rigid: Marcus would stay locked up until he could show ninety consecutive days of positive behavior, after which he could be transferred to a Positive Peer Culture (PPC) group treatment setting. Corrections staff were clueless about Marcus's background of abuse. No mental health services were provided in prison either, although he was assigned a prison "counselor" who was a veteran guard without formal training.

Marcus was both intelligent and illiterate, but he did not receive special education. Marcus hated the residential school and tried to get kicked out of class. Remarkably, he had a huge range in IQ scores, from high nonverbal intelligence to remedial verbal skills. Neither the teachers nor other staff in the youth prison had much knowledge about the origin of his problems, but this was not their focus. "Safety" was the stated concern, which meant locking up anyone who showed challenging behavior.

Marcus was highly alert when checking out whether people were friend or foe. He formed close bonds with a few favorite staff—joking, warmly asking them about their children, and giving them his drawings. But with adults he didn't trust, he prepared for battle. Most staff feared Marcus because he was "crazy" and "unpredictable," although we found him to be quite predictable. Whenever Marcus saw nonverbal cues that a person was angry or afraid of him, he would pick up any available object—clipboards, books, or pencils—to threaten them. Consistent with regulations, these threats were "major rule violations" and earned solitary confinement for a day or more.

Even when locked in his cell, Marcus kept breaking rules. He would shout sexual insults at male and female guards that he thought didn't like him. Some of his misbehaviors were sexualized, like climbing up the basketball backboard and mooning the people below. He also made a home-made "shif," or knife, in his cell and then gave it to the guards, telling them, "You don't search cells good enough"—another major rule violation. The more Marcus misbehaved, the more he was punished; the more he was punished, the more he misbehaved.

Marcus was not alone in his war with guards. Kids in the youth prison formed a gang and strongly supported any defiance of

adults. In time, Marcus and a half-dozen other youth, who also had serious problems, were being locked-down twenty-three hours a day for days on end. Most, like Marcus, were Native Americans, but all the guards were white. Untrained and frustrated, some guards called them "little pukes" and threatened to send them to adult prison where they would be raped. One guard drew a small circle and a larger circle and told Marcus "this is the size of your a--hole when you go into prison, and this will be the size when you leave."

The youth prison was a tinderbox of tension. One evening, the boys figured out how to override the electronic locks. They opened their cells, locked guards out of their dayroom, and flooded and vandalized the place to protest "being treated like sh--." The videos of the riot showed Marcus skating in the water and mooning the camera, which was recording evidence for his subsequent prosecution. The riot ended as a counselor talked the boys back into their cells. The governor arrived on the scene and was greeted by shouted curses from youth in other cellblocks. He held a press conference and, with flourish, announced that the perpetrators were rapists, robbers, and scum.

Marcus and three other ringleaders were charged with prison break, riot, and destruction of state property. Marcus was tried in adult court where the prosecutor argued that the boys had failed to use the "opportunities" provided by the juvenile system and should be sent to adult prison. However, an understanding judge ruled that the state had failed to provide programs appropriate to Marcus's developmental needs and sent him to a youth treatment program instead of prison.

In this story, we see the curriculum of control carried to its ultimate absurdity. Most people who work with troubled youth care deeply about these kids and are not abusive. But we certainly must say such abusive treatment is not rare. Volatile kids put under the control of untrained adults is abuse waiting to happen. When the inevitable occurs, our most emotionally damaged youth are blamed, which seems to justify even more toxic doses of punishment.

James Gilligan of the Harvard Center for the Study of Violence notes that people who are treated cruelly do not have to face responsibility for their actions because they have a ready excuse for continuing violence. He believes that a humane environment is required to heal violent people. Punitiveness exacerbates aggression. Gilligan concludes that the level of violence measures the community's lack of love.[12]

Flight: Boundary Building

I don't even have the time to tell you, much less
talk to that raving loony in there. An absolute
lunatic, he is.

—A therapist who had given up on Will, *Good Will Hunting*

Antisocial youth can be changed only by adults who involve
them. However, many highly trained professionals keep a wary
distance from difficult youth or act in a superior, demeaning
manner. In contrast, for two centuries youth work pioneers have
shown that these approaches are ineffective with troubled
youth. Johann Pestalozzi (1746–1827), who worked with Swiss
street kids, declared that love was the essence of education. A
century later, August Aichhorn (1878–1949) of Austria observed
that the primary unmet need of delinquents was love. Janusz
Korczak (1878–1942) of Poland and Maria Montessori
(1870–1952) of Italy championed the right of the child to be
treated with dignity and respect. These pioneers were proac-
tive, optimistic, and deeply committed to the troubled youth in
their care.[13]

The 1900s sparked major changes to the idea that children must
be submissive to adults. Youth professionals began to experi-
ment with extending respect to children. Schools were recast as
democratic communities. By 1935, there were dozens of successful experiments in empowering children in self-governance
of youth institutions.[14]

Rudolph Allers, a noted psychologist of that era, wrote that
adults who think they are superior are compelled to put a distance between themselves and the children. The principal
method they use is the withdrawal of kindness and tenderness.
Treating children with meanness and arrogance creates an enor-
mous gulf between adult and child. Adults who are insecure
demand to be treated with respect while simultaneously insult-
ing the child's dignity. Allers argued that authority must be

constructed in a child's soul, not imposed, and love is the only possible architect.[15]

Today, love talk seems naively idealistic to many. In spite of rhetoric about their importance, relationships have been systematically de-emphasized in schools and treatment settings. If powerful relationships are the foundation of reclaiming troubled youth, then arms-length, uninvolved people are by definition impotent with such youths.

Sometimes, organizational structures block bonding. Large caseloads make it difficult for many professionals to get to know individuals in their care, and much of their time is spent reacting to crisis. Likewise, factory-like schools handle large numbers of students in a depersonalized manner, managing behavior with crowd control techniques. High levels of staff turnover and the limited attention span of volunteer mentors also keep close bonds from developing. Ultimately, the most important gift any of us can give to another person is time shared in a caring relationship. People who are harried and hurried have difficulty being Good Samaritans.

Ten Myths about Detachment

Peter Benson of the Search Institute reports that avoidance of youth by adults is the norm in modern society. Eighty percent of adults avert their eyes when encountering a youth whom they do not know. Also, in typical surveys of young people, eighty percent report that adults in their communities don't care about youth.[16] Unfortunately, even people who work with difficult kids sometimes distance themselves. There are many rationalizations and half-truths that continue to increase the gulf between adults and youth. The following ten myths are some of those used to justify detachment from children.

1. Dependency interferes with self-reliance.

This myth comes from confusion between overdependency and meeting a child's needs for a secure, accepting relationship. Certainly, adults who keep a child dependent by blocking opportunities for independence are developmentally destructive. Likewise, children who are spoiled or pampered do not develop a strong sense of self-esteem.[17] However, young people need chances to make decisions and learn from their mistakes. Youth who are most secure in their relationships are also those most prepared for responsible independence. Young people who are close to adults are not stingy when expressing affection and acceptance.

2. Professional distance protects against burnout.

Many adults who once tried to build relationships with children have over the years become skeptical of such investments of time and emotional energy. Burnout is another name for loss of motivation and morale. Morale problems come from stressful job conditions and the feeling that one just is not making a difference. As a result, adults withdraw from difficult kids for self-protection. When detached staff become ineffective staff, morale erodes further.

Distrustful youth interpret aloofness as disinterest or rejection. They won't invest in adults who don't seem to care about them. For example, Jeffrey, who had been in special education and treatment programs for years, described how he purposely tried to make adults uncomfortable: "I wanted to see if they really cared; people who really care wouldn't give up even if they are uncomfortable."

3. Investing in individual children is favoritism.

Group settings require that adults realize the messages sent by open displays of special treatment. Still, the adult who says that "I treat all students the same" is admitting that treatment is not being determined by individual need. A more sophisticated model of fairness is to recognize that each child is unique and requires individual treatment. Staff can personalize greetings and interactions without causing the youth's peers to feel jealous or rejected.

Most adults are likely to have better relationships with a specific type of children. In one training activity, we ask staff to select the type of youth they most enjoy serving: aggressive, depressed, dependent, or passive-aggressive. Staff go to one of four marked stations in the room to show their preference. Each type of youth usually has some adult fans. For adults, it is a personal and professional challenge to be effective with a wide range of behaviors.

4. Closeness risks sexual boundary problems.

At a time when allegations of abuse are common, there is an understandable fear of crossing sexual boundaries or becoming overinvolved with a particular youth. As a result, some professionals avoid ever physically touching a child in case it is misunderstood. Certainly this is an important issue, particularly with children who have histories of physical or sexual abuse. Yet these young people desperately need models of appropriate relationships, especially close emotional and even physical nurturing, to contrast their abuse experience.[18] Whether physical touch is appropriate is a complex issue that depends on the setting, age of the youth, and other variables. Even if children should not be physically touched, however, they need adults who will touch their lives. Emotional closeness must meet the needs of the child, not the needs of the adult.

5. Detachment is a sign of professionalism.

Professionals who are positive and go the extra mile for a youth may be subject to criticism from those who think objectivity requires a detached view like that of a scientific observer. But this "outsider lens" limits adults to information that can be gathered from surface behavior. Albert Bandura suggested that it is also important to understand the private logic that an individual gives events.[19] This understanding requires an insider view. If we do not listen and empathize, we may miss half of the data.

A related concern is that if adults invest in a youth, they will become advocates instead of impartial professionals. On this count, we plead guilty. Young people who have been hurt by adults need to know that an adult is on their side.

6. Youth would rather talk to peers than to adults.

Do kids really want adult help? Will they listen to us? As they mature, youth reach beyond their childhood dependence on adults to bond with peers. Yet, it is a mistake to assume that youth believe peers are always the best source of information and support. A major study showed that while teens tend to go first to peers for advice, they don't fully trust the advice they receive. Overwhelmingly, the youth surveyed said that they would prefer the maturity of parents or other adults. However, youth often don't feel that they have a relationship with adults that allows them to talk openly about their problems.[20] Youth without Family Privilege who have not learned to trust adults are particularly in need of the wisdom that can only be provided by an adult mentor.

7. Relationships are not part of the job description.

"I am here to teach, not wet-nurse students," said one secondary teacher. While children are whole people, some modern professionals provide narrowly specialized teaching or treatment interventions that poorly meet the child's real needs. The French term *professionale deformation* refers to this kind of blindness.

Waln Brown of the World Organization of Resilient Kids reflects on his own experiences as a troubled youth.[21] Although his case records list numerous contacts with psychologists and psychiatrists, clinicians who just produced pessimistic diagnostic reports didn't connect with him. Brown notes that one court worker, who was less than well trained, maintained an ongoing relationship and correctly decoded the meaning of Brown's behavior. The classic role of the therapist as neutral and uninvolved is being challenged by studies showing the importance of engagement, spontaneity, mutuality, and authenticity.[22] Similarly, effective teachers with at-risk students are able to win over those who previously have hated teachers.

8. Social distance is necessary for discipline.

Attempts to create an authoritarian image are seen in the stern appearance of prison guards and the behavior of strict teachers. However, a colleague who is captain of security in a large federal prison says that the most dangerous security situations result from highly hostile relationships between guards and prisoners. Such opposition results in angry pride and residents who are motivated by little else than plotting against their hated captors.

Genuine authority is earned only by showing respect, even to disrespectful people. Social control comes from social bonding. For example, in Marcus's story earlier in this chapter, when youth rioted and took control of a cellblock in a youth prison, the governor called out the National Guard. Still, the person who talked the youth back into their cells was a counselor who residents believed cared about them.

9. Children with attachment disorders can't form genuine bonds.

Attachment disorders are believed to result from severe interruptions in the parenting process.[23] In pop psychology circles, it has been chic to put the labels of *attachment disorder* or *kids without conscience* on a wide variety of adult-wary children. We are highly uncomfortable with derogative terms that hint at the genre of *psychopath*. Generations of therapists have used such labels to diagnose and discard people who did not leap onto the therapy couch. We have worked with hundreds of youths whose files were drenched in similar pessimistic predictions. Such reports should be treated with maximum skepticism since they often set in motion a self-fulfilling prophecy. Why would we waste time trying to relate to a kid who is incapable of attachments? These youth might better be understood as suffering from what Levy in 1937 called "affect hunger," which is a desire for affection and love.[24] The obvious solution: feed them.

10. Disrespectful kids don't deserve special attention.

The difficult kids who need the most attention can also be the most unpleasant to serve, so it is easier to spend time on people who appreciate our efforts. Adults in charge of troubled children are sometimes trained by the youth to keep their distance. For example, parents may stop trying to monitor the youth's activities outside the home in the hope of avoiding confrontations with the teen. Adults ignore negative behavior as they escape into an "out of sight, out of mind" mentality.[25] Families who resist treatment intervention also train therapists to keep their distance.[26]

Not everybody hates or hides from difficult kids, and we applaud the many professionals and volunteers who break the barriers to closeness. In one rural Michigan school, every staff member from elementary through high school agreed to serve as a mentor for one student at risk of failure. Their goal was to insure that these students had at least one advocate throughout the school year. Other schools are forming "connections committees" to reattach troubled students to the school.

Millions of mentors are connecting to individual children and teens. Scott and Hanne Larson work in youth prisons from Maine to Minnesota. They train volunteers from faith communities to mentor incarcerated youth and carry those relationships back into the community. The night we visited their Massachusetts program, Scott took us to Boston Commons where troubled youth were handing out sandwiches to homeless people. The Larsons call their therapeutic philosophy "reparenting," which is not much different from the original Latin term for education: *educare*.

Fool: Manipulation Games

It's a poker game with this young man. Don't let him see what you've got.

—Gerald Lambeau, Will's math mentor, *Good Will Hunting*

Poker may be a popular card game, but in real life trickery makes for poor relationships. Youth who are skilled at deceiving adults can easily trap them in manipulation contests. Distrustful young people are very wary of any adult who seems to be trying to deceive them.

To manipulate is to manage or influence skillfully. Properly understood, manipulation is a sign of strength and the basis of all effective behavior since humans first manipulated tools to survive. What gives manipulation a bad name is when people handle each other in a manner that deceives or damages them in some way. When a person has a pattern of using others without concern for their feelings or rights, it suggests limitations of conscience. In its extreme form, manipulative people are sometimes called "sociopaths."[27]

"Manipulation" is a highly overused label for behavior that bothers adults. For example, six girls in a South Dakota correctional facility were shackled and locked in cells twenty-three hours a day. When the girls cut themselves in desperation with glass from a broken fluorescent light, their behavior was called "manipulation." Likewise, boys from the same facility, who had suffered similar segregation, tried to cut or strangle themselves—more "manipulative" behavior according to prison officials.

Deceiving the Deceiver

Austrian delinquency pioneer August Aichhorn (1878–1949) described the most challenging youth as impostors because they are skillful at hiding behind masks and fronts that conceal their real selves from others.[28] Traditional management approaches backfire with the impostor: The authority figure is only an enemy to be outwitted, while permissive adults are weak and easily abused. Likewise, traditional therapy gives the impostor a stage on which to pretend to be a patient.

Just as angry youth draw adults into cycles of aggression, so impostors suck adults into manipulation contests. In 1949, Hoffer contended that relationships don't work with these "psychopathic liars and swindlers" so one has to beat them at their own con game. He called this "deceiving the deceiver" and speculated that Aichhorn's success with these youth was due to the fact that the old man was a better trickster than his boys. Hoffer thought that the basis of Aichhorn's method was to pose as a powerful and superior impostor.[29]

As described by Hoffer's theory, Aichhorn seems little more than a Machiavellian tyrant. One might assume he would applaud boot camps where drill instructors intimidate, disorient, and overwhelm delinquents to teach them discipline. However, Aichhorn's own writings prove that this interpretation is wrong. In 1907 Austria, this twenty-nine-year-old elementary school teacher led the fight against military models for maladjusted boys. He organized his own homes and schools based on "a practical psychology of reconciliation." As the McCords document in their classic book *Psychopathy and Delinquency*, Aichhorn saw love as necessary for change:

> Aichhorn based his therapy on affection: "We must make good on the love of which he has been deprived." Once rapport had been solidly established, the staff increased their demands upon the boys. They criticized and imposed social controls. Using the affectional bonds, they apparently brought the boys to a new sense of social responsibility. Aichhorn reported that his aggressive boys acquired new tolerance for frustration and new consciences.[30]

There is little doubt that Aichhorn used *positive* manipulation. He put thieves in positions of trust. He arranged it so that a youth who was comfortable hurting others would experience guilt. Most importantly, Aichhorn projected a quality that school discipline researchers call "with-it-ness."[31] Students knew they couldn't easily fool him and probably thought he could read their minds as well. However, his influence (manipulation) was not designed to disempower youth but to neutralize their negative manipulation and offer chances for positive choices. To avoid being controlled by youth, Aichhorn sometimes operated in inconsistent and unpredictable ways, but his commitment to their well-being was never in question.

Paradoxical Treatments

Youth are programmed to be independent, and they resent it when they think someone is trying to control them. Adults are the same. So it is not surprising that there is interest in paradoxical techniques that promise to outgun those who try to manipulate us. The philosophy behind paradoxical manipulation is to make people believe they are acting freely so they have less motivation to be resistant.

Milton Erickson and Jay Haley developed paradoxical strategies to stop clients' manipulations.[32] For example, parents of a ten-year-old boy took their son, a chronic bedwetter, against his will to see Erickson:

> The boy's parents brought him yelling into Dr. Erickson's office. When the boy paused to catch his breath, Dr. Erickson told him to go ahead and yell again. After the boy yelled and paused to take a breath, Dr. Erickson yelled. The boy turned and looked at Dr. Erickson and was told it was his turn to yell.[33]

Such techniques cleverly lock the child in a double bind. He either quits screaming or he does what the doctor says. These methods may prevent power struggles with children, but they border on deception and lose their effectiveness when the youth figures out what the adult is doing. The limits of paradoxical methods are most obvious when they backfire and are used by young people against adults. For example, fifteen-year-old Kevin told us how he outwitted staff who were apparently using paradoxical treatment tricks:

They tried reverse psychology on me. If I had trouble with the group, instead of punishing me, they would say, "Oh, it is too stressful. We will give you your own staff." They took me to the nicest day room in the facility with a TV, couch, everything. They thought they could trick me into wanting to go back with the group. I just played video games all day and watched TV. It was a blast.

A common paradoxical technique adults use is to act as if they are not bothered by negative behavior. If the youth is trying to upset the adult, this strategy removes the payoff, and it certainly beats counteraggression. Of course, a youth like Kevin can also use this technique of fake indifference: "They had point sheets for prizes and treats. I thought this was bullsh—, but they could trick the little kids with it. I said I didn't care if I got points."

Paradoxical methods often include *embracing* the undesired behavior. When the adult seems to permit problem behavior, it becomes less attractive. A different paradoxical technique of *overcorrection* requires the youth to repeat the undesired behavior, presumably to give the youth control over the behavior while making him or her sick of it: "Since you enjoy swearing so much, please spend five minutes shouting out all the swear words you know."

Another paradoxical technique is *predicting relapse*: "In my opinion, you will not be able to quit using drugs." The resistant youth is challenged to prove the therapist wrong. Whether this strategy will discourage a youth or become a self-fulfilling prophecy is an open question.

Aichhorn also sometimes used paradoxical treatment but in a positive sense. He would put untrustworthy students on their honor. When a mother brought her son to be interviewed by Aichhorn, she angrily scolded the boy for being an incurable thief. Aichhorn handed the boy a large bill and asked him to go to the store to make a particular purchase. The lad was in a double bind: If he stole the money, he proved his mother right. But, he returned with the purchased item and the proper change. This method has the advantage of demonstrating trust. But leaving money around to teach honesty to thieves has its limits.

Since paradoxical techniques aim to minimize defiance, they are attractive to professionals and parents, but whether they actually give freedom and self-control is another issue. If the method requires that the adult use lies and deception, the strategy can be expected to interfere with the development of trust.

Provocative Therapy

Perhaps the most intrusive manipulation game is deliberate provocation. With this technique, instead of avoiding conflict, one incites it. Provocation is sometimes used with young children thought to have attachment disorders. The adult sets up a power struggle with the child and deliberately escalates it to physical restraint and "holding." The unproven theory is that evoking rage and catharsis will cause "bonding" to the controlling adult. Tragically, kids have suffocated while being restrained or wrapped tightly in blankets during such "attachment therapy." Why one would anger a child to gain the child's love is a mystery, especially to the first author who had attachment problem labels in his case files.

With older youths, provokers use different methods. For example, the principal in the movie *The Breakfast Club* challenges the delinquent student, Bender, to punch him; Bender must either back down or get beat up by his principal. In another example, staff at a residential treatment center gave youth some distressing news (which was not true) to see how they would handle a crisis. Similarly, a boot camp kept youth in the dark for months about when parents might visit in order to "create anxiety."

We recently met a social worker who was using "provocative therapy" with youth by "getting in their face" to see what kinds of frustration they could handle. When we challenged his methods, he referred us to an aging treatise on the topic. The book carried the theme that if the therapist isn't entitled to use most of the same techniques available to the patient, the contest will be unfair and there will be little motivation for change.[34]

Almost anything goes in provocative therapy if one can show that it is done in the pursuit of treatment goals. The therapist may tell obvious lies or do crazy and zany things to keep the patient from controlling the relationship. In such a setting, it is not unusual for a therapist to call a patient names, presumably in good, caring humor and designed to jump-start therapy. For example, an obese patient might be called a "blimp" and a female with an attitude a "slut." The patient's angry response to the insults is met with sarcasm:

> Client: (Angrily, loudly) You'd better quit talking like that or I'll . . .
>
> Therapist: (Interrupting . . .) If you want to throw a temper tantrum, why, go ahead, be my guest. . . . Why, hell, here at this hospital we have what I call a temper-tantrum room for people like you who *need* to have temper tantrums. Actually, the rest of the staff call it the seclusion room, but I think temper-tantrum room sounds better, don't you?[35]

Presumably, when humor and caring smooth these abrasive confrontations, some patients may benefit. But confrontation has two strains, one benign and the other toxic. Confrontation can mean facing a person with the truth, but it also means an attack. In provocative therapy, any method, short of murder, probably could in theory help somebody. By this ethical standard, the end justifies any means.

"This Is for Your Own Good"

Most attempts to outwit troubled youth are not creative or, even at first glance, controversial. Many programs use kindly coercive control systems. Often, severe punishments are softened by professional euphemisms. A lock-up is called a "quiet room" or "meditation room." Children who misbehave are restricted from basic developmental activities and then told, "This was your choice." Failure to cooperate in therapy or fill out "thinking error" logs can lead to major restrictions. In essence, these coercive methods deprive youths of the chance to learn from their mistakes—and then blame them for their lack of responsibility.

Ira Schwartz, former head of the Office of Juvenile Justice and Delinquency Prevention, described a coercive program in an adolescent psychiatric unit. These are excerpts from an information sheet given to youth upon admission to show what was expected of them:

> The code system is a program to help us learn about your behavior and allow you to earn privileges. You will be on a code where you can do what is expected of you and where staff can watch over you until we know you better. The staff and doctor will decide where you start. This will be decided when we know why you are here and what your behavior is like.
>
> A staff person will talk to you and tell you about the codes and what you need to do. They will answer any questions you have. Once a staff person has talked to you, it is up to you to follow the rules and ask any questions if you are unsure of what to do.
>
> You can then work at going up the codes as you begin sharing about yourself, following the rules, and being responsible for your behavior. Code raises will be up to the staff and your doctor and will be given only when you are following through with the program at the code you are on.
>
> You can also go down the codes. Some of the reasons could be: not following your code; out-of-control behavior; running or trying to run away; or having drugs, weapons, or tobacco.[36]

This example is a reasonably harmless system of control, no doubt refined through attempts by youth to find loopholes in these rules. The adults who wrote these policies are presumably trying to be positive while they tell young people, "This is for your own good." But, as a colleague asks, "If what we are doing for them is so good, why are they fighting us so much?"[37] Paulo Freire observed that some of the most effective systems of oppression are created by people who are well-meaning.[38]

Nothing is gained by letting children outwit adults. In fact, these young people need adults who are strong role models and who exercise authority in a respectful manner. Attempts to deceive, provoke, or coerce a youth can easily cross over into disrespect. These strategies also represent the Pessimism Lens.

Manipulation games are played on slippery slopes. There is nothing wrong with "manipulation" when it refers to the ability to manage or influence skillfully. But such interventions must be fair play, namely honest and prosocial behavior. This definition rules out lying in any form. Otherwise, manipulation results in a young con artist admiring an older, more talented one.[39]

PADD: A Blueprint for Failure

A major study of troubled youth conducted by the University of Michigan showed that it was not the type of prior delinquency that predicted success but rather the nature of the relationships between adults and youths.[40] Adults who gave young people high expectations, autonomy, and care had very positive impact on student adjustment. Adults with low expectations, coercive management styles, and detached relationships drove youth deeper into negative peer subcultures.

Youth are unimpressed by credentials but can quickly decide whether an adult is a friend or foe. When preparing this book, we turned the diagnostic tables and asked youth from troubled backgrounds to describe the type of adults who are likely to fail with adult-wary youth. The youth had little difficulty identifying the behaviors of adults at risk of failure in this work. They described behaviors related to adversarial relationships that are similar to behaviors identified by empirical and clinical research. Their responses fit into three recurring patterns of behavior: pessimism, antagonism, and detachment. Here are some typical comments:

Pessimism

◆ My sister was wild, so teachers think I will be, too.
—Ramon

◆ I got a look at my file. It said I had been "irretrievably damaged." —Carlita

Antagonism

◆ Staff are always trying to play mind games with us. —Lorraine

◆ Many adults look down on kids and think they can boss us around. —Mike

Detachment

◆ I can tell if a person is just there for the money. —Rachel

◆ I had lots of counselors, but our eyes seldom met. —Waln

Since there are diagnostic manuals for kids who can't successfully cope, we think there should be a way of identifying adults who can't give help. Such a profile would be useful in selecting professionals or in retraining those already working with youth. This profile could be could be called PADD, which is an acronym for Pessimism Antagonism Detachment Disorder. Below is a possible checklist for this "disorder":

Pessimism Antagonism Detachment Disorder (PADD)
Adults at Risk of Failure With Challenging Youth
Pessimism

- Assuming the worst. *You'll probably screw up.*

- Underestimating talent. *You'll never amount to anything.*

- Flaw-finding. *What are you hiding?*

- Blaming. *You have a rotten attitude.*

Antagonism

- Superiority. *You are just a kid.*

- Manipulation games. *Don't think you're fooling me.*

- Coercion. *How dare you defy me.*

- Punitiveness. *I'm going to make you pay.*

Detachment

- Mechanized management. *Just do what you're told.*

- Label instead of understanding. *You're nothing but a troublemaker.*

- Lack of concern. *It's a waste of time talking to you.*

- Zero tolerance. *You're out of here.*

Following the procedures used in diagnostic checklists, one could identify specific signs and symptoms to make a diagnosis. We might also invoke the zero-tolerance standard, namely, one bad mark is too many. Of course, we present the PADD profile with tongue slightly in cheek, but its validity is based on the expert opinions of youth who are masters at finding adult weaknesses.

On a positive note, we believe this condition to be "treatable." Such is the focus of the following chapters.

Endnotes

[1] Lewis 1997.

[2] Covey 1990.

[3] Males 1996.

[4] Branden 1994.

[5] Long, Fecser, and Brendtro 1998.

[6] Patterson, Reid, and Dishion 1992.

[7] Brokenleg, Van Bockern, and Brendtro 1999, 4.

[8] Knitzer, Steinberg, and Fleisch 1990.

[9] Tutu 1999.

[10] Skinner 1989.

[11] Montgomery 1997.

[12] Gilligan 1997.

[13] A discussion of pioneers in youth work is found in Brendtro, Ness, and Mitchell 2005.

[14] Lhotzky 1994.

[15] Allers 1934.

[16] Benson 1997.

[17] Coopersmith 1967.

[18] Finkelhor 1979.

[19] Bandura 1982.

[20] Larson and Brendtro 2000.

[21] Brown 1997.

[22] Safran and Muran 2000.

[23] Allen and Land 1999.

[24] Levy 1937.

[25] Barkley, Edwards, and Robin 1999.

[26] Patterson and Fopgatch 1998.

[27] Palmer 1974.

[28] Aichhorn 1935.

[29] Hoffer 1949.

[30] McCord and McCord 1956.

[31] Kounin 1970.

[32] Erickson 1980. Haley 1973.

[33] Maag 1996, 222.

[34] Farrelly and Brandsma 1974, 57.

[35] Ibid., 60.

[36] Schwartz 1989, 140.

[37] Durkin 1988.

[38] Freire 1970.

[39] Treischman, Whittaker, and Brendtro 1969.

[40] Gold and Osgood 1992.

chapter four

Pathways to Opportunity

Sean: He just sat there and counted the seconds until the session was over. It was pretty impressive, actually.

Lambeau: Why would he do that?

Sean: To show me he doesn't have to talk to me if he doesn't want to.

—*Good Will Hunting*

By age twelve, I had lots of experience fighting teachers, foster parents, counselors, and psychologists. I had successfully sabotaged fifteen placements in foster homes and institutional settings, about one every three months. My court worker, Mr. Jackson, lost all patience and sarcastically offered me a choice: be sent to an all-girls boarding school in Cleveland or to Starr Commonwealth for Boys in Michigan. In my equally sarcastic response, I chose the girls school. It was not to be. Having burned all my bridges in Ohio, Mr. Jackson transported me to Michigan. After a six-hour drive, I arrived at Starr Commonwealth, a residential school for troubled boys.

I tried to talk Mr. Jackson out of taking me into the admissions building. That didn't work, so I decided to try a new tactic. Larry Brendtro was the first person I met. When he tried to conduct the admissions interview, I refused to talk. He peppered me with all the tricks of his trade. Instead of responding, I gave him the stony, silent treatment, rejecting his best attempts at rapport-building. He smiled, asked me about my interests and my family, and told me about Starr. I snubbed him.

In my mind, Brendtro was like everyone else that I had met in my life. He was not to be trusted. He was nothing more than an obstacle to be overcome, someone to mislead, toy with, and dispatch of, just as I had done with dozens of other adults. He was just another nosy person trying to control me and take away my freedom.

After nearly an hour of facing down this latest enemy in my war with the world, I was pleased with my performance. Tiring of this game of "therapeutic chicken," however, I finally blurted out my only words of the interview: "I won't talk with you, and I won't stay in this goddamn place." I refused to be admitted to Starr. A small victory was at hand.

"Ha," I thought to myself, "once again these people have proven no match for my stubbornness and resolve, just f--- them all." Mr. Jackson was disgusted and swore at me as we got back into the car, but I was so ecstatic I didn't care. I was going back to Cleveland!

The return trip was very quiet except for the music from the radio. Mr. Jackson did not say much after his outburst, for which I was glad. I felt very much at peace. It was dark out, the car sped along, and as far as I was concerned, all was right with my world. I had gotten my wish to return to Ohio. I savored my victory, because I had learned to appreciate small triumphs. There

*had never been any big triumphs. However, too soon I lost
the battle.*

*I had purposely tried to ruin any chances for admission to Starr in
my first visit. Thus, I was devastated just days later to find myself
once again in a court vehicle being taken back to Michigan. Of
course, I knew what I had to do—run away or cause enough trouble to get kicked out. But Starr was sending students to The
University of Michigan Fresh Air Camp on a lake with waterskiing,
so I decided to wait until after camp to run away.*

*When our bus approached the camp, we read the sign and dis-
covered we were in the town of Hell, Michigan. Ironically, while
camping in Hell, I made my first human connection since being
torn from my family. His name was Mr. Lambert, and he was a
recent college graduate who didn't have enough good sense to
know that kids like me are hopeless.*

*I didn't meet Mr. Lambert under the best of circumstances. I had
nearly drowned while trying to water-ski, and when he
approached me, I was furious and embarrassed, swearing and
sulking on the shore. He tried to cheer me up and soon got me
involved in a baseball game where I restored my lost dignity. I
decided not to run away just yet. In time, my bond with Mr.
Lambert would extend to others. But I was very selective, still
fought teachers, and was not interested in school.*

*Growth comes in spurts, sometimes with setbacks. Starr provided
a stable environment for me, which included the things that normal teens do. I went to high school, played sports, ate pizza with
my friends, and went on dates. I was safe. Even if I showed my
worst side, these people didn't give up on me. When I was sixteen,
I received my driver's license. Later, my Starr roommate and I
"stole" our group home's car for a few hours of joyriding. Before
we could return, we were arrested and spent the night in the city
jail. I was petrified. If there ever were a time that Starr would
kick me out, this would be it. However, in the morning I was
released and they warmly welcomed me home like a prodigal son.*

Not long after I was arrested, Larry was finalizing his book
Positive Peer Culture *with Harry Vorrath when he plopped the*

manuscript in front of me for my opinion. The studied delinquency expert was asking for help from the real expert! I felt respected and validated. As I read the manuscript and made suggestions, I was performing meaningful work. Larry also benefited by gaining my opinion.

Small seeds can have great yields. Whether seeds of ridicule or respect, each lay down deep roots. Many people planted seeds in my life. Our housemother, Mrs. Loken, was a retired missionary. With her regal but earthy personality, she had the backbone to guide and nurture troubled teens. Coheading our surrogate family was twenty-one-year-old youth worker Marty Mitchell. Because he was closer to our age, we didn't always see him as an authority, but he was a model of what we someday might be. Who ever would have imagined that Marty and I would both receive doctorates from the same university while studying under the same advisor. Marty was also a coauthor of my first book.[1]

My closest friend at Starr was Michael. We had a lot in common. His mom had tried to kill herself and succeeded. Once she was gone, he found out his dad wasn't really his father either. Unlike my game of anger and resistance, Mike tried to please and excel. Sometimes, I thought he was a brownnose. I figured that he was a fool for trying to get close to adults; surely, he would only get burned. In another sense, maybe I wished I could be more open like he was. We both had lost our brothers, so when we found one another, we became like brothers—even after we both left Starr.

In time, as my distrust slowly decreased, I finally understood that I belonged, that I had a family. My surrogate father was Mr. Lambert. During vacations when other kids went home, I sometimes spent time at a lake with him and his extended family. This was the first stable family I had ever seen at close range.

When I graduated from high school, I left Starr for college. For most kids, this is a time of triumph as they try to be independent of their families. For me, it was a time of terror, for once again I was about to be abandoned.

The Opportunity Lens

As we discussed in Chapter Three, when seen through the Pessimism Lens, problems are disasters. Seen through the Opportunity Lens, however, problems are opportunities for positive growth and development. While not minimizing the seriousness of problems, the Opportunity Lens sees them as challenges for learning instead of proof of damage and defect.[2] The Opportunity Lens stops hostile relationships with youth and instead has them join a helping alliance. This new approach—also known as resilience, positive psychology, and positive youth development—has only recently begun to accumulate its own literature.

Changing the old ways is difficult, and the Pessimism Lens is still alive and noisy. Media headlines scream that we are being brutalized by super predators, punks, and thugs. As a result, many people view troubled youth from difficult backgrounds as outcasts rather than as heroic young people struggling to overcome overwhelming odds.

For the last fifty years, we have been flooded with fancy and professional-sounding names for pathologies and disorders, including negative labels like dysfunctional, deviant, disruptive, disordered, and disturbed. Then, like sloppy scientists, we made uninformed conclusions and created simplistic treatment interventions that only addressed superficial symptoms. At its core, this approach focused on fault-fixing and blaming. Rarely did we search for the strengths in children.

The focus on fault-fixing turned attention away from the obstacles many children face within their own communities. As a society, much of what troubled us in young people were symptoms, and our strategies focused on symptom reduction. We used labels like drug users, pregnant teens, school dropouts, gang members, and thugs. Driven by outrage and fear, we used billions of dollars to launch attacks on these symptoms while ignoring the underlying issues.

Even if fault-fixing worked, giving a youth a problem-ectomy would not prepare him or her to be a healthy, successful member of society.[3] Negative labels are powerful messages that can influence attitudes, behavior, beliefs, social policy, and resource allocation. The Opportunity Lens requires changing descriptions of children to positive terms and using labels such as "at-promise," talented, gifted, and filled with greatness.[4]

For over a hundred years, the great pioneers in work with wayward kids have tried to lead the way from pessimism to hope. In 1909, social worker Jane Addams wrote of the spirit of youth in the city streets.[5] Years later, psychiatrist Karl Menninger attacked his colleagues for "furor therapeutics," saying their focus was like that of a surgeon confusing a tray of bloody tissue with a human being.[6] Educator Anton Makarenko called for creating schools of joy.[7] Psychologist Nicholas Hobbs said his profession needed to change from a preoccupation with deviance to the celebration of strength.[8] But old ways die hard.

Recently, some professionals have started to realize, finally, that labeling, punishing, controlling, blaming, reducing symptoms, and treating problems without seeing or addressing underlying issues was not working so well. In fact, it was failing. Many began to say, "What would happen if we looked for strengths, met developmental needs, created opportunities for all kids to connect to a positive caring adult, and created safe environments for our children?" Indeed, what would happen? This question—this small, logical idea that seems too obvious to have been ignored for so many years—is catching the fancy of educators, human service professionals, policy makers, and communities. It is an idea whose time has come.

Many children of adversity become strong by developing their inner resources and finding support from positive adults and peers. We call these youth resilient, because they spring back from trouble. The more we study resilience, the more we see that the potential to overcome difficult odds lies in all young people.

The pioneers in studying resilience were Emmy Werner and Ruth S. Smith. Their groundbreaking thirty-year study of children from disadvantaged families on Hawaii's island of Kauai yielded surprising results. Instead of succumbing to risks such as parental psychopathology, alcoholism, and poverty, many children were thriving and maturing into successful, happy adults.[9]

Resilient people are those who can survive risk and overcome trouble. In our own way, each of us is a survivor. None of us is a stranger to stress. Some people like Steven Callahan, who was lost at sea for seventy-six days, survive through heroic action. To his rescuers, who called him a superman, Callahan said, "I kept struggling to survive not because I was heroic, but because it was the easiest thing for me to do, easier than dying."[10] Most survivors have less dramatic tales of long-term battles against the stresses in their lives.

Stories of survival and resilience are often gripping, uplifting, and inspiring. Whether fact or fiction, such stories can be personally transforming, calling us to our higher, better selves.[11] Survival stories, like resilience research, challenge us to build strengths and supports in all our youth, particularly those who lack hope or purpose. We should not be lulled into the belief that resilient survivors are perfect heroes who support themselves to beat the odds. We are all responsible for getting involved in the lives of youth in order to change the odds. Resilience is not a constant characteristic but how one interprets one's own life. A key factor in resilient people is a confidence that the odds can be overcome.[12]

Resilience as a characteristic probably varies from person to person. However, some of the literature distinguishes between *internal strengths*, which are characteristics of resilient youth, and *external supports*, which are protective factors that encourage resilience.[13] Internal strengths include intelligence; imagination; a likable personality; the ability to set goals; a sense of purpose; the ability to form close, positive, personal relationships; and a sense of spirituality.[14] While some of these characteristics are innate, many can be gained by experience.

External supports are almost too obvious to be listed, yet many of our youth do not have these supports. Resilience is nurtured by a safe environment, at least one adult who is strong and consistently caring, schools that hold high expectations and believe in youth, parents or other caregivers who acknowledge their accomplishments, positive peers, and opportunities for young people to serve.

Protective factors decrease a person's susceptibility to risk factors.[15] For example, children living in a threatening situation may thrive in spite of stress if they connect with teachers, coaches, clergy, neighbors, or other adults. These adults provide support, set positive expectations, and encourage the child as he or she seeks a purpose in life.[16]

Studies at the Search Institute have shown that children whose developmental needs have not been met may turn to a wide range of high-risk behaviors. In order for such children to turn their lives around, adults must strengthen the *Developmental Assets* that affect these youth.[17] The Search Institute has identified forty such Developmental Assets, which include both external supports and internal strengths. Instead of looking at risk and dysfunction, the focus shifts to the question, "Why do youth succeed?" It is in that spirit that the science of positive youth development has emerged.

Positive Youth Development in Reclaiming Environments

Positive youth development (PYD), strength-based approaches, and community involvement in the lives of young people are gaining popularity. More and more, communities are embracing PYD as an alternative strategy to cope with our concerns about youth. Reed Larson notes:

> We are often more articulate about how things go wrong than how they go right. . . . We have numerous programs aimed at curbing drug use, violence, suicide, teen pregnancy, and other problem behaviors, but lack a rigorous applied psychology on how to promote positive youth development.[18]

PYD helps youth become physically and emotionally healthy, well-rounded young people who are able to build relationships, develop positive leisure activities, and gain social, academic, and employment skills. Positive models do not ignore the importance of treatment and intervention when necessary; these approaches are complementary. However, we expect less need for intervention and treatment as more and more developmental programs are available.

PYD is an ongoing process in which young people are involved with caring adults. Creating opportunities for youth has to be explicit and intentional. More importantly, PYD combines community involvement, community ownership, community mobilization, and youth involvement. This approach is less focused on holding agencies responsible for the well-being of our children and more interested in changing conditions in the community to foster healthy youth development.

This change in focus reinforces the idea that kids grow up in communities and that if one child is at risk, then all children are at risk and live in at-risk communities. It recognizes that young people are the product of those communities and reflect the health of those communities. This approach also puts the focus where it belongs: on creating nurturing communities and not on blaming victims and fixing faults. We all have a stake in healthy communities so we can have healthy young people. As Hugh Price, President of the National Urban League, observes, "Youth development is what we do for our kids on a good day."[19] We might add that all days should be good days.

Peter Benson, president of the Search Institute, has promoted the idea of community alliances around youth issues. These alliances should include businesses, churches, educators, child welfare and human service professionals, government, and foundations.

Elsewhere we have written of the many ways that faith communities can become an extension of families and parenting.[20] Communities of faith support youth with cross-generational bonds of love, the foundation of all Family Privilege. How better to replace pessimism with hope than by drawing on our spiritual heritage? Families should be central in this process, and we need to return to tribal views of family as a network of people who act as relatives to one another. Family is not just a matter of genetics but also of emotional bonds. Benson concludes that we are all responsible for unclaimed children, for all kids are our kids.[21]

From Adversary to Ally

Who is on my side? Who?

—2 Kings 9:32

The secret to success with rebellious youth is to enlist them as allies. Such youths bring a long history of conflict with authority, and the burden is on the adult to help overcome their distrust.

A century of research and practice in education, treatment, and youth development firmly establish the important role of positive relationships as a requirement for success.[22] While a positive relationship is not itself enough reason for change, the absence of such a relationship can sound the death knell to success. Sigmund Freud (1856–1939) recommended that therapists be sympathetic in order to be associated with "images of people by whom [the patient] was accustomed to be treated with affection."[23] Easier said than done, said Winnicott, who contends that even the best-trained adult will have "love and hate reactions" to the difficult behavior of these individuals.[24]

A positive relationship is essential in treating and educating challenging youth. This respectful alliance involves a shared vision and the building of a positive emotional bond.[25] The single most important factor in successful therapy is the quality of the alliance between the helper and person being helped.[26] Trust is more important than technique.

In a therapeutic and respectful alliance, adults and youth cooperate to solve a problem, such as relieving a crisis or pain, or to achieve a common positive goal, such as building strength. It is essential that efforts be made to build this positive alliance when young people offer an opportunity. Too often, therapy involves a professional asking probing personal questions before trust has been built. Not surprisingly, this search for problems and pathology often meets only resistance.[27] The following paragraphs compare the adversarial encounter to the respectful alliance:

> *The Adversarial Encounter.* The young person does not trust the adult. In the young person's view, the adult doesn't genuinely care or understand. In such an encounter, youth and adult become opponents, working at cross-purposes. The adult tries to gain control over the youth while the young person strives towards autonomy. The mutual hostility leads to detachment and avoidance.

> *The Respectful Alliance.* The young person believes the adult is worthy of trust. In the young person's view, the adult genuinely cares, understands, and is able to help. Trust is the foundation for working together. As youth and adult join in solving problems and pursuing positive goals, a spirit of cooperation develops. The mutual respect increases communication and social bonding.

The adult helper's opinion of the relationship is a less reliable predictor of success than the opinion of the person receiving help.[28] Perhaps the most important factor is whether the helper is in an "I'll fix you" role or whether both parties work together, sharing responsibility in a joint struggle to solve important problems.[29] The ideal alliance is a cooperative partnership, not a powerful expert treating a passive patient. The respectful alliance is also essential in forming partnerships with parents. Family therapists who do not build collaborative working relationships actually make matters worse for troubled kids.[30]

It is not simple to change conflict into positive bonds. Even strong alliances may experience one or more "ruptures," and when these occur, it is important to heal this "relationship decay."[31] Bronfenbrenner notes that every child needs at least one adult who is irrationally crazy about him or her.[32] But one adult may not be enough with an extremely guarded youth, since the risk is high that the relationship may fall apart in a time of crisis. Airplane pilots always use back-up navigation systems in case one instrument fails. Similarly, we should protect against relationship problems by establishing backup attachments.

Figure 5 contrasts adversarial encounters with respectful alliances.

Figure 5

Adversarial Encounters

Distrust
Youth does not believe adult genuinely cares, understands, and can help.

Antagonism
Youth and adult at cross-purposes. The adult seeks control, the youth autonomy.

Detachment
Mutual hostility increases avoidance and social distance.

Respectful Alliances

Trust
Youth believes that adult genuinely cares, understands, and can help.

Cooperation
Youth and adult work towards common goals and mutual problem-solving.

Engagement
Mutual respect increases communication and social bonding.

Adversarial Encounters

- Often defies authority.
- Argues with adults.
- Is deliberately annoying.
- Blames others for their own mistakes.
- Is touchy and easily annoyed.
- Is angry and resentful.
- Loses temper.
- Is spiteful and vindictive.

Respectful Behaviors of Youth

- Usually cooperates with authority.
- Asserts without hostility.
- Is considerate of others.
- Takes responsibility for behavior.
- Is tolerant and accepting.
- Is friendly and good-natured.
- Manages angry feelings.
- Is generous and forgiving.

Adversarial encounters fuel adversarial youth behavior. In contrast, respectful alliances promote respectful youth behavior. The adversarial behaviors listed in Figure 5 happen to be the diagnostic criteria for Oppositional Defiant Disorder.[33] The respectful behaviors are simply the positive counterparts to the oppositional behaviors.

We are not implying that oppositional behavior is the product of some adult failure. By its very nature, however, oppositional behavior requires an opponent and adults too often fill that role. When students display chronic oppositional behavior without adult provocation, they have a well-entrenched pattern of private logic and personal motivation for fighting adults. As established in research by Dodge, often this pattern is related to a tendency to blame hostility on others.[34] His study shows that these youth understand hostile or harmless behavior in general, but not as it applies to them personally. Presumably, they have interpreted life events to suggest that it is wise to be suspicious, distrustful, or paranoid about the motives of others. As Aaron T. Beck says, they become prisoners of hate who look at their world with the private logic of "let me count the ways you've wronged me."[35]

Youth who have not been treated with dignity become indignant. Children who have not experienced benevolence are on guard against malevolence. It is too simple to assume that distrust is a personality trait that cannot be changed. Instead, the adult must help young people examine their private logic and coping strategies.

Adults who fail to form an alliance are likely to use behaviors of "belittling and blaming" and "ignoring and neglecting."[36] Although the potency of the alliance is well researched, much more work needs to be done to develop techniques to improve alliances.[37] While the qualities needed for working with difficult youth can't be taught, we believe it is possible to shift from adversarial to respectful alliances.

Savage or Survivor?

To illustrate the stark contrast between the Pessimism and Opportunity Lenses, we turn to the book *Savage Spawn: Reflections on Violent Children*, which was written by California child clinical psychologist Jonathan Kellerman.[38] Best known as an author of crime novels, Kellerman tackles the nonfiction topic of youth violence, offering stories and research tidbits penned with a pessimistic spin. Using clever rhetoric that would be applauded by those who demonize delinquents, the book focuses on so-called psychopaths, who are described in a chapter called "A Species Apart" (p. 18).

The Boy in Business

The *Savage Spawn* poster boy is thirteen-year-old Tim, a youth seen for two sessions by Dr. Kellerman. Tim's case history shows that his elderly grandmother has been raising him since he lost both parents in an auto accident when he was eighteen months old. The grandmother is referred to Dr. Kellerman (we will call him Dr. K), who sees patients at night. Dr. K's notes on the meeting with the grandmother are as follows:

> I met with Grandma alone for a history-taking ses-
> sion. Her initial descriptions of Tim's behavior set
> off no warning signals. The boy didn't "mind," was
> lax about cleaning his room. Bright and a quick
> learner, he refused to do his homework, was per-
> forming below capability, wasn't affected by her
> attempts at discipline—scolding, yelling, withdraw-
> al of privileges, occasional grounding (p. 7).

When Dr. K. asks Grandma if Tim is bothered about the loss of his parents, her eyes well up with tears remembering her son [Tim's father]. She says, no, Tim never asks about his parents. Dr. K.'s impression is that grandmother is deeply concerned about Tim's problems but she projects an air of "profound inep-titude" (p. 6) and is ill-equipped to raise a teenage boy.

The chapter on Tim begins with the bold declaration: "THIS KID SCARED ME" (p. 5). Tim is a tall, muscular, tan, good-looking, well-dressed youth who might easily pass for sixteen. He wears conservative clothing uninfluenced by youthful fash-ions. With a ready smile, Tim gives the doctor a hearty hand-shake and then offers him a black business card on which Tim's name and address are engraved in silver. "He sat down opposite me, crossed his legs, stretched, grinned again, said 'Nice place,' with all the casualness of a drinking buddy" (p. 10). Already, we can infer that Tim is comfortable with male adults, and Dr. K. is not comfortable with Tim.

"Nice card," Dr. K. says. "Got to have one if you're in business," responds Tim (p. 10).

What follows is a cat-and-mouse game where Dr. K. tries to find out just what business supports the lifestyle of this well-dressed boy with smooth social skills. Tim plays word games with the doctor but doesn't tell.

> Tim pulls out cigarettes and asks to smoke but Dr. K. prohibits this. Tim immediately shifts to a strategy of shrugs and silence, fending off the doctor's questions. Frustrated, Dr. K. confronts Tim about not obeying his grandmother. Tim shoots back, "She's a stupid a--hole. Doesn't know what's flying. She's old" (p. 12).

The doctor interprets Tim's comments about his grandmother as "vicious" and plans his "next move" with this youth who presents himself as "street-wise, cool and collected" (pp. 12–13). He decides to broach the topic of Tim's deceased parents. Tim jumps up and pulls out an expensive leather billfold to show a snapshot of a good-looking couple in their twenties. "Major piece of a--, huh?" Tim says, describing his mother to the incredulous doctor (p. 14).

Tim has only one more session with Dr. K. during which he boasts of having had sex with a dozen girls, claiming he often collects their panties to sell to other boys. His braggadocio "clogged the room" (p. 14). Tim says school is stupid and he intends to be a "big businessman" (p. 15). At this point, the doctor abandons his earlier hypothesis that Tim might be inwardly troubled: "There was no wall of defenses. He had nothing against which to defend because he was truly untroubled. Completely different from the other noncompliant boys I'd seen. It was as if I were sitting across from a member of another species" (p. 15).

Tim has the ability to intimidate Dr. K. by subtle behaviors. Such interactions marked their second and final session. Tim renews his request to smoke and is again refused. He narrows his eyes into slits and stabs a "hateful smile. . . . He spread his legs. Touched his inner thigh briefly. Winked" (p. 15). Dr. K. doesn't tell the reader what he made of this seductive behavior except to say, "I reminded myself he was only thirteen" (p. 15). On this note, this adversarial evaluation ends. Dr. K. observes:

> When he left, I made sure he exited first. He knew
> I was watching his back. Stopping at the door of
> the waiting room, he made a sudden move with his
> shoulder, as if about to butt me. I recoiled. He
> checked the movement, a classic bullying tech-
> nique. *Faked you out.* Then he turned to me.
> Winked again (p. 15).

Tim never came back, and his grandmother did not return Dr. K.'s calls. He heard that she had moved to another city hoping to place Tim in a boarding school. Based on two sessions, the therapist classified Tim as a psychopath:

> I encountered a few, mercifully few, other boys like
> him. All displayed the same emotional flatness, lack
> of conscience, grating bravado, inflated self-esteem,
> ambitious pleasure seeking. All disparaged those
> who loved them. All had engaged in criminal
> behavior. Some had already been incarcerated.
> None cared to change. None changed (p. 17).

The therapist lost track of Tim but concluded that "most proba-bly he's done terrible things" (p. 17).

A Failure to Connect

Of course, we haven't met Tim. Perhaps he *has* gone on to do terrible things. We doubt it. But if we interpret Tim's story from a strengths perspective, Tim might easily be described as a sur-vivor instead of a savage. For example, when Tim shows a photo of his deceased mother and describes her as "a major piece of a--," this could be Tim's badly chosen, macho manner of expressing pride in his mother. However inappropriate, this com-ment could provide a way for the therapist to connect with Tim.

We have used Kellerman's account of Tim in workshops on principles of strength-based assessment and intervention. We initially ask participants to counter the pathology perspective of *Savage Spawn* by trying to identify Tim's possible strengths. Their list always fills a flip chart. Then, having established that Tim has talents, we discuss what went wrong in the relationship between Tim and Dr. K. In order to trust Dr. K., Tim would have to believe that he genuinely cares, understands, and can help him. The foundations of this trust are discussed briefly below:

Does the youth believe this adult genuinely cares?

In his own words, Dr. K. described this case: "Call him Tim. I've forgotten his name, but Tim will do fine" (p. 5). Dr. K. most enjoyed working with patients who had "*real* problems. . . . After all, I was a medical school professor, had no desire to be a high-priced babysitter" (p. 6). While Tim certainly had real problems, something about this boy rubbed the therapist wrong from the start.

Studies show that when helpers dislike the people being helped, they typically shift from supporting and encouraging to belittling and blaming. Most helpers are aware of their dislike of the person, but mistakenly believe they can still treat the person fairly.[39] However, children and youth can usually tell whether or not the adult cares for them by decoding subtle verbal and nonverbal cues.

Does the youth believe this adult understands?

Kids who don't trust adults build elaborate masks to hide who they really are. By his own account, Dr. K. seldom had encountered a kid like Tim. Strong academic credentials alone may not prepare anyone for the challenge presented by someone like Tim. On the other hand, appropriate clinical and life experience could prepare a parent, teacher, or counselor for connecting with a child like Tim. Still, even a licensed pilot should not attempt to fly an unfamiliar plane in bad weather. Could it be that the therapist read the instruments wrong and became disoriented? Instead of seeking more information to understand this complex youth, the therapist makes quick judgments based on superficial behavior as interpreted with textbook ideas about psychopaths.

A young person's worldviews may be radically different from the helper's notion of reality. If the adult responds in a way that causes the youth to feel disrespected or disgraced, communication will shut down. Understanding a youth means discovering his or her private logic and worldview. When the helper knows the youth's "psycho-logic," as Dreikurs calls it, the adult is prepared to help him or her find a way of thinking and acting that will better meet his or her needs.[40]

Does the youth believe this adult is able to help?

From their first meeting, Tim was in charge and the therapist was on the run. Once he discovered that he could con and control Dr. K., Tim realized he was unlikely to get help here. Tim dodges the therapist's questions with humor and word games. When angered, Tim uses an intimidation strategy called "woofin'" in street vernacular, employing a threatening tone and body language.[41] Tim doesn't need to say "f--- you," instead he encodes hostility in subtle sexualized gestures. Even as he exits—with the therapist cautiously walking behind him—Tim lurches in sham aggression. "Faked you out."[42] As one teacher participating in a discussion of Tim said, "In more ways than one."

What would it take to reach a youth like Tim? Someone who remains positive in the face of hostility. Someone who recognizes Tim as the best authority on Tim. Someone who, even if intimidated, stands courageously beside this boy. These are the prerequisites of creating a respectful alliance.

Connections, Continuity, Dignity, and Opportunity

When designing appropriate treatment for youths like Tim, we use four principles of PYD, which we call CCDO:

- **Connections:** *Social bonds to family, school, peers, and community.*

- **Continuity:** *Patterns of thinking and coping that influence life pathways.*

- **Dignity:** *Environments that cultivate trust, talent, power, and purpose.*

- **Opportunity:** *Situations that develop strengths, supports, and goals for positive growth.*

The CCDO principles can be used with all ages and in a range of settings including education, juvenile justice, treatment, and family- and community-based youth development. CCDO is a blueprint for strength-seeking instead of flaw-fixing interventions. The goal is to create environments in which all youth can thrive and grow.

Decoding Behavior

Dr. K. had almost no insight into Tim's life but concluded that Tim was probably a hopeless case. Tim has the expertise on himself that nobody else does. Our approach with such young people is to enlist them in the adventure of discovering how they have come to this point in their lives and where they are going. Telling their life story is the core of the process we call the Developmental Audit.[43]

When an airplane crashes, an elaborate system is available to determine the causes of the disaster in order to prevent recurrences. But when a youth is seriously failing, we have had no similar system. Reclaiming Youth International has created the Developmental Audit to meet this need.[44] The Audit uses CCDO principles for assessment and treatment planning. Audits are used with youth whose serious problems make them a challenge to schools, courts, treatment settings, and community agencies. This investigative tool helps us understand what happened and why. The Developmental Audit has been used with a variety of problems such as threats of school shootings, special education assessments, school expulsion hearings, court deliberations, and repeated failure in treatment or foster care placements.

Searching for Strengths

A popular commercial was once developed for the United States Army. The commercial focused on finding hidden strengths in potential recruits. A young man is shown playing video games and an ominous voice-over says, "Sam likes to play video games all day. What kind of future is there in that?" The enthusiastic answer is that Sam can have a future flying the new and highly video-like aircraft of the technologically advanced U. S. Army. In today's Army, Sam's problems are seen as assets.

Using a term coined by Peter Benson of the Search Institute, CCDO is a framework for looking at "developmental assets."[45] The Developmental Audit also provides a new approach for reaching challenging young people like Tim who do not respond to flaw-finding methods. Using the case of Tim, we will illustrate how a Developmental Audit might shed light on his self-defeating behavior.

Thirteen-year-old Tim had obvious strengths, but Dr. K. only saw manipulation and deficits. Tim uses tactics to intimidate, avoid, and trick others who try to understand him. Tim will not let down his guard to any adult on a flaw-finding expedition. Instead, we approach him with great respect, for he is the world's only expert on Tim. He can teach us about his connections, significant life events, and his strengths and needs.

In a Developmental Audit, we are like scientists who observe carefully, pose questions, and search for possible hypotheses to explain puzzling behavior. Following the CCDO framework, this is what we want to discover:

Connections: Who are the significant people in the youth's life?

Young people develop in an ecology of family, school, peers, and community.[46] We know almost nothing of his world outside the therapy office, but Tim gives many leads to explore. When Tim calls his grandmother a "stupid a--hole," does he really despise her, or could he be using this shocking language to get the therapist to mind his own business? Perhaps it is a way of saying that she is well-meaning but not meeting his needs. Having already lost both parents, does Tim fear that Grandma will also

die and leave him totally alone? Could it be that Tim is bothered by never having known his parents but doesn't raise this
topic with Grandma because it will only upset her? If so, then
Tim may be concerned about her feelings. Are Tim's abilities to
engage adults and his attempts to impress them a way to manipulate or a search for relationships? Who gave Tim this confidence? Where did he learn to act like a "drinking buddy" of
older adults? Businessmen exchange calling cards but why
would a thirteen-year-old boy? Does Tim have any friends his
own age? With whom does Tim spend his time, and what does
he like to do? When life gets difficult, to whom does Tim go for
support or is he a loner? Does Tim have any other significant
community connections?

Continuity: How has Tim coped with the challenges of his life?

Tim clearly has the intelligence to share stories about the most
important events in his life. He has already provided several
topics that could be further explored. What was it like growing
up without parents? What challenges has Tim faced and how
has he dealt with them? If we probe for problems, he will shut
down. If we can focus on his strengths and the difficulties he
has surmounted, however, he will not be threatened. We listen
for clues to answer the questions in our mind. Grandma didn't
describe Tim as running the streets, so is he really as "street-
wise" as the therapist presumes? Where would a well-dressed
kid like Tim hang out on the streets? Tim boasts of having had
sex with many girls, but would he really share intimate information with an adult he doesn't trust? What experiences with sex,
alcohol, and drugs might this smart, good-looking, charming,
lonely kid have encountered? Tim says his grandmother "doesn't
know what's flying"; could this mean he hides his troubles from
her? If she is so "profoundly inept," how did she raise such a
smart boy? We would want to know what insights and concerns
she has about Tim. Tim bristles at being controlled. What angry
encounters has he had with teachers or authorities? What was
Tim trying to prove in these confrontations? As Tim sees that
we are trying to understand him instead of blame him, he will
gain more courage to share what is important to him.

Dignity: How can adults help Tim develop strengths and self-respect?

Tim projects an air of self-satisfaction but does he really believe he is a person of worth? Does he really feel that he is significant, competent, powerful, and a good person? He holds adults at bay, but does he hunger for a mentor or a father figure? Does Tim really disrespect his grandmother or is he perhaps helping to support her emotionally or financially? If it is true that Tim has casual sex with many girls, does he have a genuine relationship with a girlfriend? Tim has considerable intelligence, but when did school quit being important in his life? What passions or activities might capture the interest of this intelligent youth? Tim says he wants to be a businessman, so what jobs might he have experienced or be interested in pursuing? Does he have dreams and goals, or does he live one day at a time? Tim tries to control adults, but does he feel in control of his own life? Tim projects an image of not being bothered by troubles, but is that just a way of pretending to be strong and covering his weaknesses? Does Tim see any purpose to his life? Is he totally egotistic or are there ways that he shows consideration and respect for others?

Opportunity: How can adults help Tim in building his future?

Tim has the ultimate responsibility to set the future course of his life. Adults have the responsibility to support and encourage him in this journey. Opportunity is the forward-looking dimension of the Developmental Audit. Here we bring all of the elements together: building opportunity includes cultivating *social bonds, inner strengths*, and *positive self-worth*. Using the following Circle of Courage model, Tim should develop ways to meet the four universal goals for developing healthy youth:

- Belonging: Children need opportunities to experience secure, loving relationships in order to believe "I can trust others."

- Mastery: The potentials of children must be developed through opportunities to learn and succeed in order to believe "I have talent."

Figure 6

Art by George Blue Bird is reproduced with permission of Circle of Courage, Inc.

121

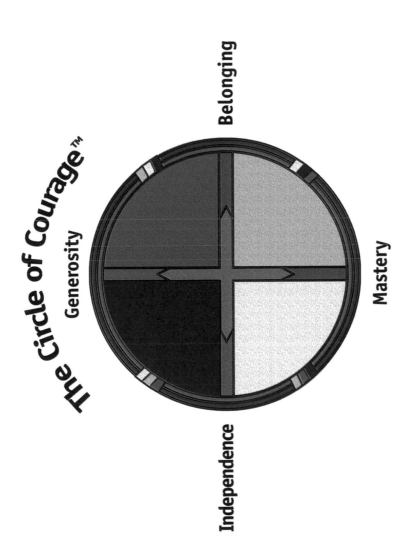

The Circle of Courage™

Belonging

Generosity

Mastery

Independence

- Independence: Children must be given opportunities to develop responsibility in order to believe "I have power over my life."

- Generosity: Children must be given opportunities to contribute to others in order to believe "I have a purpose for my life."[47]

Of course, the big question remains: Who is this boy with the black business card? One hypothesis produced by each group of professionals who have studied Tim's story is that he could be a male prostitute; many of the clues are consistent with such a lifestyle. However, there are other possible explanations that might explain Tim's behavior. Even if Tim is involved in illegal or promiscuous activities, he still has the potential to do something of value with his life. Tim might even become a great therapist someday. Presumably, he would not be fooled so easily by kids who have learned to outwit adults.

Winning Trust With Wary Kids

"What you see is what you get" does not apply to the behavior of a guarded youth like Tim who masks his real self to hide what is in his heart. Adults who cannot see beneath surface behavior have little influence with adult-wary youth. However, clumsy or premature attempts by adults to break down a youth's defenses may produce attacks, avoidance, or other defensive strategies. These behaviors protect a psychologically fragile person, and battering them down can cause emotional damage.[48] While it is not always possible or wise to ignore these behaviors, adults should not expect to have a strategy for every act of defiance. To a youth who sees adults as enemies, these battle plans make sense. While we must manage the short-term surface behavior, the long-term solution lies in changing the distrust with which the youth views the world.

As trust develops, much defiant behavior will be abandoned, although supportive confrontation still may be needed. The confrontation must be handled with concern and compassion, challenging the behavior while embracing the youth. The goal is to have the youth examine whether these defensive strategies are still necessary. It is almost impossible to create a respectful alliance with a distrustful youth in a hostile environment. These youth are very good at catching the subtle cues communicating hostility. While any relationship is bound to be rocky at times, it is critical to repair these ruptures and build good will and respect. However frustrating the behavior of a youth, the effective adult helper is one who honestly enjoys interacting with the youth. In 1913, William James gave this advice in his *Talks to Teachers*:

> One hearty laugh together will bring enemies into closer communion of heart than hours spent on both sides in inward wrestling with a mental demon of uncharitable feeling. To wrestle with a bad feeling only pins our attention on it and keeps it still fastened in the mind.[49]

Good-natured humor lowers the barriers of distrust and eases bonding and communication. For example, Natalie had experienced repeated rejection but learned to force a smile to cover her feelings. We made no mention of this until some trust was established. Then, catching her in one such smile, we said, "Natalie, you have this fantastic smile, and it seems that whenever you want to hide what you feel, you flash it. That must really throw people off the track!" Natalie then gave us a genuine smile of acknowledgement. Thereafter, when she began to revert to her smiling mask, she would usually catch herself and say, "Whoops, there I go, hiding behind my smile again!" A former defense became a shared bond of humor.

Another example is provided by Darrell, who gave us a powerful account of how hard it is to move from distrust to trust. Darrell is a thoughtful individual who contributed his ideas for this book. From childhood, he experienced a series of tragic losses that, in his words, "left a hole in my soul." Subjected to violence, Darrell became very guarded with people, and he particularly distrusted psychologists, who tried to force him to revisit his painful past. But Darrell greatly enjoyed training horses. He noted, "Both people and horses who have been abused see humans as dangerous. It takes lots of courage to trust and become vulnerable when you have learned that humans are predators."

Darrell called our attention to the fact that in *Good Will Hunting*, the psychologist, Sean, is first seen lecturing his college class on the topic of trust. Darrell also noted that the central theme in the movie *The Horse Whisperer* is trust. Wild or abused horses see humans as predators and react with flight or fight strategies. Monty Roberts, whose life inspired *The Horse Whisperer*, learned how to read the body language of horses and calm those that had been abused. Rejecting traditional methods of "breaking the will" of wild horses, he worked instead to "gentle" them. He achieved this by "joining up" with the horse, creating a natural bond that communicated trust.

After learning to "gentle" the most damaged horses, Roberts and his wife used similar trust-building methods with youth, opening their home to over forty street kids damaged by drugs, abuse, and a host of social problems. The key to overcoming distrust, according to Roberts, is to abandon the outdated practice of "you do what I tell you or I'll hurt you." Threatening, intimidating, and inflicting pain may result in superficial behavior changes, but trust creates a much more powerful contract. Stated in simplest terms, trust is built by communicating the message "I am an ally and not a predator."[50]

Endnotes

[1] Seita, Mitchell, and Tobin 1996.

[2] Wolin and Wolin 2000.

[3] Pittman and Irby 1996.

[4] Seita, Mitchell, and Tobin 1996.

[5] Addams 1909.

[6] Menninger 1963.

[7] Makarenko 1976.

[8] Hobbs 1994.

[9] Werner and Smith 1977.

[10] Callahan 1986, 340.

[11] Burns 1988.

[12] Cohler 1987.

[13] Rhodes and Hoey 1994.

[14] Blom, Cheney, and Snoddy 1986. Brown 1983. Everson 1994. Rhodes and Hoey 1994. Seita 1994.

[15] Benard 1997. Benson 1997. Werner and Smith 1992.

[16] Benard 1997.

[17] Benson 1997.

[18] Larson 2000, 170.

[19] Cited in Newman, Smith, and Murphy 1998.

[20] Larson and Brendtro 2000.

[21] Benson 1997.

[22] Brendtro and Ness 1983.

[23] Freud [1913] 1958, 139–140.

[24] Winnicott 1949.

[25] Martin, Garske, and Davis 2000.

[26] Docherty 2000. Gaston 1991.

[27] Hubble, Duncan, and Miller 1999.

[28] Goldstein, Heller, and Sechrest 1966.

[29] Greenspan and Cullander 1975.

[30] Huey et al. 2000.

[31] Safran et al. 1990.

[32] Bronfenbrenner 1986.

[33] American Psychiatric Association 1994.

[34] Dodge 1993.

[35] Beck 1999.

[36] Henry, Schacht, and Strupp 1986.

[37] Horvath, Gaston, and Luborsky 1993.

[38] Kellerman 1999. (Note: The page numbers for quotes from this book are in parentheses in the text itself.)

[39] Henry, Schacht, and Strupp 1986.

[40] Dreikurs 1964.

[41] McIntyre 1996.

[42] Kellerman 1999, 15.

[43] Wood et al. 1999.

[44] Reclaiming Youth International 2001. [Note: Developmental Audit is a trademark of Reclaiming Youth International, which provides training and certification in this process.]

[45] Benson 1997.

[46] Bronfenbrenner 1979.

[47] The Circle of Courage Model is described in Brendtro, Brokenleg, and Van Bockern 2002.

[48] Clark 1998.

[49] James 1913, 201.

[50] Roberts 1996.

chapter five

The Courage to Change

Do what's in your heart, son. You'll be fine.

—Sean Maguire, Will Hunting's therapist, *Good Will Hunting*

My life after Starr Commonwealth was not easy. The transition to independence is difficult for many but was especially so for me, since I lost my most important connections. There were no phone calls from home, because there was no home. There were no requests for care packages, for who would prepare and send them? There was no one to ask for money, and there was no one to help me navigate the confusing and complex world of college. There was no one to cheer me on, or if necessary, to kick me in the rear when I fell behind in my studies.

Once again I plunged into crisis. Poor grades led to academic probation, and I dropped out of college. I worked for a time at a foundry in blazing heat and polluted air. While I made good money, I found new motivation to return to college. Back in school, I had more rocky years, but when I became a youth worker in a residential facility, I knew I was contributing to others. Finally, my life seemed to be coming together.

There would be another major speed bump on my road to stability. Mr. Lambert, my Rock of Gibraltar, died. I had feared this was coming. "D," as I now called him, had separated from his wife. I had heard that "D" was depressed over the breakup of his family and had moved back home with his parents. I knew firsthand the pain of losing a family, so I called him long-distance to offer support. He told me that he had thought of running his car into a highway bridge abutment but had ruled out suicide since he wanted to see his two boys grow up. I was stunned to hear "D" considering killing himself. I suggested that we should get together, but he backed away. After that phone call, I was consumed with worry and helplessness. I also wondered how I was ever going to be successful if someone of his caliber could not overcome life's difficulties.

I received a phone call from Starr informing me that "D" had died. My hope was that it was an accidental death, but "D" had killed himself. His funeral was like the finale to every abandonment in my life. In the following months, I found myself driving around in my car, thinking about his death, the meaning of life, and why these kinds of things happened. I looked over at the empty passenger seat and engaged in hypothetical conversations about my life and his life. I would tell him what I was doing now and share my hopes and dreams. I imagined that he would be proud of me for following in his footsteps and working with youth and that he would share his fatherly wisdom about my career and my life.

Sometimes experiencing a great loss or defeat helps us reflect on the real meaning of our existence. Will Hunting destroyed many relationships, but the major cause for his change was the loss of his girlfriend, Skylar. I pushed away many would-be fathers, but it was the death of the man who taught me what a real father was that allowed me to do what was in my heart. A tragic past does not need to seal the fate of any person. Even the most painful experiences can help a person choose new pathways.

It takes many years of successful independence for those of us who grow up as troubled kids to be able to leave our past behind. Many other former troubled youth who are now *successful professionals say that although they have survived, they still have scars. Some harbor hatred and bitterness, but I do not believe that we must lead scarred lives. Like others who have faced adversity, it is possible to become stronger having survived.*

I have developed a whole series of tools that allow me to over-come the past. The most essential of these are my spiritual anchors and my attachments to the important people in my life. I spend a lot of time reading, reflecting, and thinking. I try to keep my internal core intact even if the world is swirling around me. Sometimes I feel like an ice cutter, trying to plow through all of the obstacles in my way. It helps to be creative, to look at things from different points of view, and to find the positives in bad luck. I believe I have succeeded in developing what the Wolins call "survivor's pride."[1]

In Don Quixote, Cervantes writes, "The entire sum of existence is the magic of being needed by just one person." Today, by this measure, I am doubly blessed with a loving wife, Lori, and a daughter, Anorah. Our little girl has taught me as much about the larger spiritual lessons of life as I have taught her about practical skills of coping with the world.[2] Her love is transform-ing, and her wonder and imagination have forever touched me. At my side through challenge and celebration has been my wife, Lori, the patron saint of strength. She has supported and encour-aged me even when I was unaware that the darkest midnight soon would fall to the brilliance of a rising sun.

Hemingway once said, "Life breaks everybody, and then some become strong at the broken places." This belief is echoed every day in the lives of young people who show the resilience of the human spirit. However, in every community, every neighbor-hood, and every school, there are children who face adversity unprotected and alone. Courage to survive in a dangerous world comes from strong human bonds and a commitment to some great cause beyond ourselves. No longer can we allow any child to face life's struggles without support or to navigate life's path-ways without a purpose.

Challenge and Change

In a classic work on therapy, Schulman notes that a young person who has experienced rejection and abandonment needs a positive, restorative relationship with a caring adult to balance the effects of earlier rejection and abandonment.[3] This relationship can only happen if the helping adult is a trustworthy authority figure who will not abuse the youth. Trust not only requires becoming vulnerable but betting that the trusted person would never purposely cause hurt.

Humans need predictability so that they can establish patterns of thinking and acting that are stable and resistant to change. Still, many difficult children abandon their established but troublesome behavior in adolescence or early adulthood. New challenges and relationships call for new patterns of coping. As a result, many delinquent youth settle down when they enter the adult world of work and family.[4]

There is a vigorous debate between researchers who see life pathways as fixed and those who think they can be changed. For example, Olweus predicts that half of young bullies will become adult felons.[5] In contrast, Werner and Smith estimate that over half of children from highly troubled backgrounds adjust in adulthood.[6] These scholars are looking at the problem from different viewpoints; there are paths of resilience as well as paths of trouble. We might call this looking through the Pessimism Lens or the Opportunity Lens.

Even among those who care about children, there is a distressing tendency to give up on our most seriously troubled youth. Abandoning kids is an ethical issue since there are now a number of promising techniques for reversing problem behavior. Studies by the Office of Juvenile Justice and Delinquency Prevention show that even violent youth have potential for rehabilitation. However, the practice of imprisoning such youth often results in increased violence.[7] By their very nature, young people are still highly impressionable and adaptable, and there is no shortage of examples showing that even the most difficult youth have been able to turn their lives around and make positive contributions as adults.[8]

Problems, conflicts, and crises often result in changes to past ways of thinking and behaving. When Charles Darwin first visited Australia, he was totally disoriented by the huge variety of strange animals. From this experience, he developed his theory of evolution.

Crisis disrupts everyday life and pushes us towards new solutions. When a person is in crisis, powerful problem-solving programs trigger in the brain. Like an unsolved crossword puzzle, the problem will bother us until we figure it out. This process is called the Zeigarnik effect after the Russian psychologist who discovered the problem-solving processes in the human mind.[9]

The last time you couldn't remember somebody's name, your brain kept working on the problem—even when you were busy with other tasks—until your brain search engine found the name. When facing life problems, something similar happens. A person who can't get something out of his or her mind thinks of possible solutions, considers the problem from many angles, and then usually comes up with a new plan.

There has been much interest in identifying the stages by which people make major changes in their values, thinking, and lifestyle. Drawn from a variety of sources, here is our summary of the four steps in the change process:[10]

> *Challenged:* Challenges are landmark events that change what is normal and call for new ways of thinking or acting. These events can create opportunities as well as threats. Challenges can be uplifting peak experiences, such as becoming a parent.[11] Challenges can also overwhelm us. M. Scott Peck opens his book *The Road Less Traveled* with the observation "life is difficult." [12] Challenges that exceed our ability to cope can produce serious stress. *Physical stress*, such as hunger or homelessness; *psychological stress*, such as conflict or rejection; and *developmental stress*, such as puberty, all can create crisis. Events that bring up painful emotional memories may also trigger a repeat of past traumatic events.[13] We all manage life's challenges

in different ways. But when stress becomes too chronic or severe to manage, we can no longer use our normal methods of coping, and we are flooded by negative emotions such as fear, anger, shame, and sadness.

Contemplating: We search for a solution. Our brain locks into problem-solving mode. We look inward for possible clues and creative solutions, tapping past experience and searching our emotional memory bank. Unless distracted, we can worry day and night. Since stress also triggers attachment behavior, we also look outward to others for ideas and support. Even with distrustful people, a crisis can make them more open to help from others. Crisis arouses us psychologically and prompts us to think about our past life, our present state of affairs, and our future. In times of crisis, deep questions about the purpose of life become important, and many people search for spiritual support to help solve problems.[14]

Coping: We try new approaches. As we practice new ways of thinking and acting, we at first feel awkward and uncomfortable. If the new approaches fail, our confidence is shattered and we reenter crisis or fall back on old patterns. But if we succeed in our new role, we become increasingly confident. People need extra support at this time, and their success depends on believing that the difficulties can be overcome. If the person is using self-defeating strategies, this is an opportunity to help him or her rethink the situation and develop a better way of problem-solving.

Comfortable: If the coping methods have reduced stress or brought rewards, the person becomes more comfortable with their new behaviors. As the new ways of coping become more comfortable, the person settles into a new lifestyle. This change may be as major as a religious conversion or adopting a delinquent identity. Regardless of whether others see the new behavior as positive or negative, it is becoming part of the person's manner of thinking, feeling, and acting. People who commit to a new lifestyle often find new social groups and may distance themselves from family or old friends. These new relationships strengthen the person's beliefs and thinking patterns so that the new behavior is more likely to become stable and persistent. For people comfortable with destructive and self-defeating behavior, it may take a crisis to cause them to question their patterns of thinking, values, and behavior. For people in a positive lifestyle, such as sobriety, a crisis may cause a temporary relapse as they revert to old, established ways of coping.

As seen through the Pessimism Lens, a crisis is disruptive. As a result, interventions lean toward punishment, exclusion, and restraint. In contrast, the Opportunity Lens uses problems as the base for learning and growth.

Alliances for Growth

Many new strategies are using problems as an opportunity to create positive change. The *Resolving Conflict Creatively Program* (RCCP) began in New York City schools that were plagued by disrespect and violence. Now, RCCP extends to hundreds of sites nationwide.[15] *Discipline with Dignity* provides educators with training to shift from punishment to discipline that teaches challenging students respect and responsibility.[16] The *Positive Peer Culture* (PPC) program seeks to change negative peer cultures through problem-solving groups that build strengths and make caring fashionable.[17] *The EQUIP Program* teaches students prosocial skills, thinking, and moral values so they can help their peers.[18] The main goal in all Opportunity Lens approaches is to have adults join youth in respectful alliances for problem-solving and growth.

As we have seen, punishment and pathology-oriented approaches to troubled students often backfire, creating greater distrust and defiance. Fortunately, there are better ways to connect with youth in conflict. Life Space Crisis Intervention (LSCI) is a teaching and treatment method that was developed for precisely this purpose. LSCI helps young people examine the crises and challenges they face. By exploring significant events in their lives, youth learn to replace self-defeating private logic and antisocial behavior with prosocial and resilient coping strategies.[19] LSCI is being successfully used by counselors, educators, treatment and justice professionals, youth workers, pastors, and mentors—a full range of those who work with troubled youth in families, schools, and communities.

Children in crisis—whether angry, manipulative, anxious, or depressed—need skilled and caring adults who can help them withdraw from conflict cycles and conduct problems. Managed badly, a crisis can lead to devastating cycles of disruptive behavior and alienation. Handled well, a crisis provides an opportunity to learn new ways of thinking, feeling, and behaving.

There are many advantages of being able to talk with a youth in the moment of crisis. This experience allows us to understand the youth's characteristic ways of thinking, feeling, and behaving. Youth are treated with respect by significant adults who see them at their worst, and as a result, they learn to trust caring adults. As they become aware of their patterns of self-defeating behavior, youth gain strength-based social skills. Finally, they begin to accept responsibility for their behavior and develop positive goals for growth.

Young people often use self-defeating behavior as the result of some past trauma or crisis. To protect themselves, they adopt characteristic patterns of thinking, feeling, and behaving. Even if these behaviors are partially self-defeating, such coping methods must still provide some reward or else the youth would stop using them. It is not always necessary to learn how these patterns of problem behavior started. However, young people do need to discover that the old dangers no longer exist and there are better ways of protecting themselves and coping with the world.[20] A respectful alliance makes adults and youth partners in this pursuit.

Partners in Their Own Healing

We have found that some youths like to read books about troubled kids, particularly if they find them on the bookshelf of a teacher, counselor, or parent. Kids are fascinated by what adults are trying to do to them. We always recommend that staff share progress reports with young people. In fact, we sometimes sit down with a youth at a computer and write these reports together. Youth who are clever enough to sabotage treatment are mature enough to be involved in their treatment goals.

Not surprisingly, adults who have pessimistic views of youth try to keep progress reports and staff plans secret from youth. The result is that goals and strategies become weapons for the adults to use. However, the ability of youth to spy on staff plans is legendary. Youth tell tales of sneaking a peek at their "confidential" files as if they had succeeded on a mission impossible. Youth read every memo and policy document meant for staff eyes only. One youth told us the supposedly top-secret teacher code to be announced over the public address system in his school in the event of gun violence. Another told us how he would pore over brochures describing staff roles and philosophy for clues on fighting treatment strategies:

> Here is the packet they gave me at the psychiatric hospital. It tells what the job of the psychiatrist and others is supposed to be and what rights patients have. I need to know their rules. Then it's like being a lawyer; you use the rules against them. They also gave us this form listing ways of "breaking down walls." I studied it to get ideas on how to build walls.

An ongoing debate in education is whether schools should invite students with behavioral problems to participate in their Individual Education Plan (IEP) meetings. Some staff believe these meetings should be off-limits to students for various reasons. Adults may want to speak freely and are concerned that the information might damage students' self-concepts. Few adults wonder what the kids are thinking when a group of adults is scheming in secret about them. Other educators believe involving students will foster growth in self-awareness, responsibility, and self-advocacy. Whether youth are involved in planning their futures gets down to whether adults see them as allies with strengths or as adversaries who have little to offer.

Youth are often frustrated by not having input into the goals set for them. When treatment plans are created and enforced by adults, youth have no reason to participate. Apparently many adults think they are involving young people when they really make only minimal effort. Joe explains:

> My worker came up with all of the goals. They were written for me before I ever saw them. I was asked for input before I signed them, and I think my input was taken seriously. Still, it wasn't me coming up with the goals; it wasn't me writing them down.[21]

Unfortunately, one of the reasons adults don't listen to troubled youth is that, to quote a prominent researcher, "deviant individuals are the most unreliable informants."[22] This may be true, but the goal of all scientists is to be truth-detectors. Youth are the ultimate experts and the primary sources of information on their private logic.

Even youth with serious emotional and intellectual limitations can become skilled psychologists in their own right. Kids who have had to protect themselves from adults for years are good at defensive strategies, since for them, this is Life Survival 101. They also may be able to see basic truths that more philosophical minds might miss. After the Columbine High School shootings, a young person with a developmental disability told us, "Nobody understands why those two boys shot those other students, but I know why they did it. You just keep trying to be their friends, but no matter what you do, you are never good enough for them!" Then, with insight, this person added, "And they better quit showing this on TV or lots of other kids will be trying the same thing."

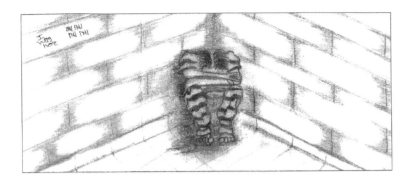

It is common in some special education and treatment settings to assume that students with developmental disabilities will only respond to simple behavioral consequences because verbal limitations make counseling counterproductive. This can be an unfortunate professional bias, because the kids may be slow but clever.

Fifteen-year-old Lawanda had been through many mental health placements and now lived in a community group home. She had a verbal IQ in the sixties and was very stubborn when staff tried to control her. She was having difficulty in school and in relationships with her peers in the group home, and her behavior was deteriorating. One evening she provoked a confrontation with a residential counselor and then ran into busy traffic. She was placed for a few days in a psychiatric hospital, and an IEP conference was held to discuss Lawanda's "impulsive, self-destructive behavior" and her "lack of cognitive control." We suggested that her behavior was intentional rather than irrational and recommended that the staff ask the other girls for their ideas about what might be bothering Lawanda. Much to the counselors' surprise, Lawanda's peers said she had spoken a day earlier of her plan to run into traffic. Feeling her life was in disarray, she had unsuccessfully tried to convince staff to put her in the psychiatric hospital for a break, something that had happened during an earlier crisis. Since persuasion did not work, she took action. Staff concluded that her behavior was not impulsive or even self-destructive, and she certainly was aware of what she was doing. Afterward, Lawanda was fully involved in educational planning and becoming a partner in her own healing.

Listening to Youth

We first met seventeen-year-old Jonathan when he gave a moving speech at a conference for Canadian youth workers. Removed from his parents as a young boy, he had spent several years in the custody of the state. In spite of hardship, Jonathan displayed remarkably resilient behavior. With humor and insight, he shared his private logic of what it was like to grow up as "property of the government" and to have no say about his destiny. Jonathan later submitted his speech for publication in a journal. His story reminds all adults to avoid relationships based on power and superiority and instead use dignity and respect.

Jonathan's Story

I know you are all busy—lots of work that demands paper, paper, paper. But I am here to tell you that I am more than a file. I am a person. I have feelings and am entitled to respect. Please don't only see the problems, see the potential.

I didn't get along with my stepfather and, between ages nine and thirteen, terrible things happened in my life, not all of them at home. I endured what my stepfather did—physically abusing me until I was thirteen. Then I decided I wasn't going to be a victim anymore. One day he hit me in the head, hard, and knocked me down, but I got back up and stared right in his face with such hate that it scared him. After that, I was taken from my home. I didn't want to live with him again. I became a PGO—which we kids in care say means Permanent Government Ownership—because it feels like the government owns us. Of course, PGO actually stands for Permanent Guardianship Order, where the government becomes our guardian until we reach adulthood.

I was an affectionate kid, but I was hurt too many times, so I turned to ice. I sometimes wish I could start my life over not knowing anybody. I have only about three good memories. I have a picture of me sitting on the lap of my dad, but when I was four, I watched my dad's death. I have always tried to figure out why he shot himself.

I blamed myself for my dad's death, but I didn't say anything about this until I was fifteen, when I asked my grandparents. I still want to know. I have always wondered that maybe I had done something to make him kill himself. I can't figure out if I was not a good kid and caused him trouble. I would have nightmares, but I didn't want to tell anybody. Even though it's a bad memory, it's my only memory of my dad, so if I shared it, it would not be my own.

After my dad died, my mother got married again. She and my stepfather didn't want to keep my eight-year-old brother, so they got rid of him by putting him up for adoption. I didn't understand at the time, but later I wondered why they didn't get rid of me as well. I haven't seen my brother since he was eight.

I was apprehended and placed in foster care before being admitted into a residential program. I lived there for eighteen months and liked some of the staff. But there are a lot of things that have happened to me in my life that I don't want to talk about. Some people who work with kids don't understand—you have to let kids connect with you and not try to force it. They sent me to psychiatrists who tried to pry things out of me, and I said, "I don't even f---ing know you, I'm not telling you sh--!"

I check out people very carefully. I am good at reading people. Sometimes I use reverse psychology, like if a counselor is getting too close, then I ask him about his life, his problems, and it scares him away. I can tell if a person really cares and wants to help or is just doing a job for the money. You know the saying: "Keep your friends close, but keep your enemies closer." If I don't trust an adult, I have to watch them even closer. I give staff respect even if they don't show it, but when they are not there, I live my life like I want. If I find a person who is open, his personality reaches my own and I bond quickly. But I don't want to talk about things that hurt. After being somebody who doesn't care about anything for so many years, it is hard to change. When I get upset, I ball things up inside, and then I finally blow up. Sometimes I hit my fist into the wall or I become violent, and then I feel guilty.

Over the years, I have had good and bad experiences in the system. The good parts have been some of the caring, trusting, and supportive people I have come in contact with. The bad parts are when people don't listen or trust me. Sometimes people disregard my say in decisions affecting my life. One of my social workers tried to run my entire life. Against my will, she made me move to a foster home in the town where my mother and stepfather lived. I was very unhappy and I begged her not to leave me there, but she made me have contact with my parents. During all of the time I was in their town, my parents only saw me five times. One time I accidentally met my stepfather on the street when I was fifteen. I was smoking a cigarette, and he began to rage at me and pushed me against a building. I thought he was going to hit me, so I hit him first.

My mother told me once if I got in trouble with the court, she never wanted to see me again. I would call her and leave messages, but she doesn't answer my calls anymore, so I quit calling. My mother chose my stepfather instead of me. After all the times I got beat by my stepdad, I have a lot of hate for him. He ruined my life, and I don't want anything to do with him. I know we will never get back together, but sometimes I think there would be a one in a million chance that we would bond like a family, like a father and son.

After being placed in foster homes against my will, I was very unhappy for the next two years. During that time I had eight different social workers. I got so I didn't care about anyone or anything. I still find it hard to trust anybody except myself, but my life is now starting to turn around. I am in a supervised independent living program and am working and completing high school. I am sharing a house with two others and I pay $400 a month rent with money that the government gives me. I am working as a chef in training. Someday I would like to be a chef on a cruise ship, as one of my other interests is marine biology. I also enjoy boxing.

I think I would like to be married some day, but I don't know if I want kids. I wouldn't want to hurt them like my stepdad did me. But little kids like me. Someone told me if you are concerned about what your parents did to you, you could change that with your own children.

For kids like me in the system, there is a lot of fear. Most kids I know don't want to talk about their problems or experiences because it will cause them more trouble. Adults need to build a bond with kids and then they will tell you if they feel they are ready. Sometimes workers lose sight of the person behind the file number. I have desires and goals, and it is important to be there in helping me achieve my potential. Some people clear the way for me and others put up roadblocks. I am the best resource you have to know and understand what is going on inside of me.[23]

Claiming Unclaimed Kids

As Jonathan suggests, the key to reaching tough kids is to see potential behind the problems. Strength-based interventions are particularly powerful with youth who have severe problems with attachment and authority. Rather than demanding obedience and trying to overpower a defiant youth, the adult tries to build an alliance with the youth. The adult is not risking his or her role as a responsible authority. Rather, the new role is more like that of a coach who guides, encourages, and demands greatness from the young person. Adults must become talent scouts seeking to find and cultivate the potentials of even the most difficult youth.

We do not suggest that these strategies are easy, but they beat battling kids. We offer the following blueprint of practical strategies for connecting with challenging youth.

1. Recast All Problems as Learning Opportunities.

Please coach me, don't scold me.

We need to shift from "crisis management" to "crisis teaching." As much as possible, we try to turn all problems into opportunities for growth. If a bully threatens a victim while other students laugh, we have a whole collection of opportunities for learning: We teach the bully positive leadership skills, the victim to be confident, and the onlookers to be responsible citizens in a caring community.

Even if students must experience negative consequences for their behavior, there is always some potential for learning and growth. When students botch things up, we are like sympathetic coaches after a losing game, figuring out what went wrong so they can win next time. This is on-the-spot social skills training as we teach them to step out of conflict cycles, to assert instead of attack, and to respect other points of view.

2. Provide Opportunities for Fail-Safe Relationships.

I need to know that you won't give up on me.

We seek to form a fan club of supporters for the youth. This small team (perhaps including a court worker, family member(s), school counselor, employer, or lawyer) can provide multiple sources of support. In the case of one boy who had been kicked out of six programs in less than two years, we formed a three person "attachment immersion team." Early in our efforts, he was almost always angry with one of us, but the team successfully reversed his downward spiral.

No young person should have to live with the terror of possible abandonment. We warn all adults who deal with previously rejected youth to avoid the kind of emotional blackmail that includes threats like "being here is a privilege, and we will kick you out if you try that again" or "no child of mine acts that way" or "I'll send you back to your father." Children need to know that even if they mess up they will not be discarded. Examples of positive messages are:

- You are my flesh and blood, and I can't let you hurt yourself that way.

- We believe in you even though you are showing you don't believe in yourself.

- We don't expect to fail with a young person who has your many strengths.

Youth must not be only the recipients of positive relationships. They also need opportunities to extend friendship to others. Programs that encourage peer and cross-age relationships provide experience in the empowering role of helping others.

3. Increase Dosages of Relationships.

I need to be sure that somebody really cares.

Adult-wary youth will not believe that we care about them without some concrete evidence. However, as children grow older, adults become less comfortable in expressing affection. Although teens cannot be physically nurtured like small children, the advance of zits doesn't mean that they don't want adult warmth. "All I want is some kind of noticement," said an angry youth in conflict with his teachers.

When communicating, we project a genuine interest and avoid "therapy talk." Giving a young person time is the best proof of genuine concern. Even when talking about serious matters, it is a good idea to find opportunities for mutual humor, since that is the universal bonding balm between humans. While public displays of affection are threatening and suggest favoritism to peers, unconnected youth are highly alert to subtle signs of special interest. Most positive interactions—such as humor, high fives, or other quick gestures of friendliness—take only a moment of time. A passing comment, such as "Wow! That's a classy shirt!" will register with students who are not used to positive "noticement."

4. Don't Crowd.

When you get too close, I need to back away for a while.

Most of us, no matter how comfortable we are with ourselves and others, have a personal space that we do not want violated. Relationship-wary youths may initially need to keep a certain "safe" distance. Not surprisingly, when adults who work with troubled youth earnestly try to begin relationships with them, the enthusiastic attempts often fail. This result is not because we do not try hard enough, but because we try too hard. We must respect the space of troubled youth. Sometimes at the very moment when a strong positive relationship is beginning, a youth will need a little time to back off. The adult should not see this as failure but as a temporary need for distance. Psychologists call this dance the "approach-avoidance" conflict.

5. Use the Back Door.

If you are interested in what I want, you are important.

Direct attempts to build relationships often backfire with adult-wary youth. But when an adult fills another less-threatening need (such as safety needs or needs for power or skills), the youth will often end up attaching to that adult. The first author gives an example:

> Mr. Lambert, who was a young youth worker when he first met me, had no training in bonding with relationship-resistant youth. Few of us do. But he reached me through the back door. He doggedly attempted to find a special interest of mine, namely my dream of being a sports hero. Although I did not trust other adults, he connected with me through a common interest. Initially, he would come to work having read about my favorite team, the Cleveland Indians. He would then engage me in good-natured fights about whether my team was as good as his Detroit Tigers. I could be argumentative and even feign hostility, but I loved it. If he had tried a "you can trust me John, tell me your problems" approach, I would have rejected him completely.

Most kids, no matter how troubled, have a special interest that may be the key to the back door. In one of our programs, a teacher had not been able to connect to a certain youth but knew he was an expert hockey player. The teacher had always wanted to own a pair of ice skates, so one day he asked the youth for his opinion about the best brand to buy.

When the youth later learned the teacher had followed his advice and bought skates, the two had something in common. We aren't suggesting going out and buying things to please kids, but rather, using normal situations to discuss some common interest.

6. Decode the Meaning of Behavior.

I try to hide what I really think.

When things are not going well or take a shift for the worse, we take an informal "ecology scan" by making a mental list of possible reasons why a student may be having rocky relationships. Questions we could ask ourselves include: Is this temporary stress, or is it an ongoing problem? Is the problem school-based, or is it a problem from home? Are there problems with peer relationships, boyfriends, or girlfriends? Is the student afraid of failure in school? Is the youth being intimidated or abused?

Unless we try to think of causes for the behavior, we are vulnerable to such naive diagnoses as "he is just being a jerk." By thinking of possible causes, we avoid personalizing the problem, and we develop a framework for understanding the troubling behavior. If appropriate, the youth might engage in this ecology scan to give us a view of his or her world. Many youth are shocked, for example, that a teacher would even care about what is going on in his or her world. When we have a better understanding of the child's worldview, we are better able to generate ideas to help decode puzzling behavior.

7. Be Authoritative.

Help me learn to control me.

Authoritative adults respect the independence of youth without abandoning their position as influential role models. They demand responsibility instead of obedience. They also are not afraid to be a leader of youth. Kids like to take advantage of adults, but they don't like adults of whom they can take advantage.

Permissive adults and bossy adults are both equally inefficient with youths who show bad behavior. Adults who make no demands are seen as pushovers. As Fritz Redl often told us, they become "friends without influence." And dictators can demand obedience, but they fail to teach inner discipline. Delinquents can become highly manipulative of people who are only interested in filling their emotional needs, and they readily reject adults who are only interested in controlling them.

Gold and Osgood found that authoritative adults who hold delinquent youths responsible while giving them some independence become more attractive role models and diminish the power of the delinquent counterculture.[24] This finding is consistent with Coopersmith, who found that parents created high-esteem kids by setting strong standards but still being open to the youth's opinions.[25] Youth are more likely to accept not getting their way if they can have their say.

Authoritative adults are secure enough not to become angry just because a young person challenges them. "I really admire your assertiveness but my decision still stands" is a much better script than "how dare you question my decision?"

8. Model Respect to Disrespectful Youth.

Your respect builds mine.

We most need to respect youth when they least deserve it. With the most disrespectful youth, we have the greatest opportunity to demonstrate and teach respect. Even if their behavior is immature and irritating, youth should not be treated as if they were small children. They do not respond to preaching, moralizing, or criticizing. Approaching a youth with respect can initially be an example for respect in return. If we accidentally offend a youth, we should offer an apology; a genuine apology is rare for youth who are used to being blamed by adults for everything.

When relationships become stormy, the distrustful youth believes he or she will be rejected. Threats to remove a youth from a program only feed the belief that, when the going gets rough, adults will give up. Often young people who say they don't care anymore are really asking whether we think there is any reason to care. They search our words and actions to discover whether we have lost hope as well.

9. Enlist Troubled Youth as Team Members.

I am the world's best expert on me.

While traditional programs do things to troubled youth, strength-based treatments see youth as partners in their own healing. Young people have rich insights into the problems of their peers, and they are our only real experts on themselves.

Professionals now have the technology to involve youth in planning education and treatment[26] and in providing treatment to their peers.[27] We often ask youth to respond to drafts of progress reports we write about them, and we even request their help in writing reports and suggesting changes. The computer offers a ready tool for side-by-side alliances. One year, at our Black Hills Seminars, a youth with a history of delinquency asked if we would write a recommendation letter for college. We sat together at a computer for fifteen minutes and produced the letter. The youth was elated to see his strengths scroll across the screen, and he continues to keep in touch while completing a college program to be a youth worker.

Students who are invited to join in meetings with parents and professionals generally handle this responsibility with surprising maturity, although the young person's agenda may not be the same as our own. Psychiatrist Robert Coles found fifth graders amazingly able to respond to such serious questions as "what about you matters most, what makes you the person you are?"[28] Adults who do not respect the opinions of young people should not expect to be taken seriously by them.

10. Touch in Small Ways.

I watch the little things you do to discover who you are.

Sometimes less is more. Periodic smaller contacts with troubled youth may make an overall impression that is far more lasting than intensive direct efforts to establish a relationship. The first author recalls:

> Many of my more memorable interactions with teachers and caregivers are incidents they have long forgotten. When Larry Brendtro was president of Starr, he encountered me in a waiting room outside my counselor's office. I sat there with pants too short, wearing what we boys called "ankle busters"—cheap, institutional socks that barely reached the ankles on my size-thirteen feet. Larry quipped that perhaps the clothing store should issue these socks to staff. Then, as if to join me in a solidarity society of the poorly dressed, he sat down and lowered his own socks to ankle-mast. There we were, the bad-socks twins, as if posed for a fashion photo for *Gentleman's Quarterly*. Larry had used humor to treat me with dignity. He does not recall the incident, but I have preserved this memory as part of my life narrative for these many years. I was touched in a small way.

11. Give Seeds Time to Grow.

Be patient with me—I am still learning.

One chronic thinking error professionals make is to assume that present problems predict future behavior. In the midst of a crisis, youths may act as if nothing we say makes sense or is even heard. Some time later, we may be surprised to discover that they remember and are able to benefit from the interaction. We often are surprised at the serious thought a young person gives to a problem, even though they outwardly appear to be indifferent or hostile.

We are born problem solvers. Given time and experience, we can surmount most challenges. Einstein wrote of the time he figured out that traditional theories of physics did not adequately explain the universe. For seven years, he was in a state of psychic tension until he finally solved the problem.[29]

Often we plant therapeutic seeds that may bear belated fruit. We know that the brain constructs our life stories by selecting and remembering crucial events that have major influences on the path of our lives. A colleague recounts that when she was a poor African American child, she asked her principal if she thought she could someday be a teacher. The woman told her she could even be a principal. Today, she has her doctorate in school administration.[30]

12. Keep Faith and Hope Alive.

I look into your eyes to see if you will give up on me.

Many youth come from backgrounds where the goal is survival rather than meeting their potential. Parents have told us, "My main goal is to keep her from getting pregnant like her older sisters" or "I just want to keep him from going to prison like his father and his older brothers." Youth who have never been given examples of success need to believe there is some potential and purpose for their lives beyond the limited horizons of their prior experience. They also need lots of nurturing and care. At the first sign of failure, they tend to switch to "underdrive" and operate on lowered expectations. Other youths refuse to give up, but it is only rebellion against adults that drives them.

We do not try to break the spirit of challenging youth but instead call forth their greatness. Youth need to understand that they are here for a purpose, that they can contribute, that they come from someplace, that they have a culture, and that they are supported by a higher power. Intuitively, youth strive for meaning, for contribution, and for greatness. Many youths need to reconnect to their spiritual and cultural roots and find a reason for living beyond themselves.

Two centuries ago, the German educator Goethe captured the essence of strength-based education: We must search for the kernel of virtue hidden in every flaw.[31] We give young people writings by those who have overcome great personal hardships, and we show them that they have many of the qualities of resilient people. We applaud their courage in the face of trouble and encourage a sense of survivor's pride. We see problems as potentials. For example, a youth loyal to delinquent friends is showing the potential for generosity. Delinquent leaders already have executive abilities and we need only alter their focus.

Never Giving Up

In a keynote address at a Reclaiming Youth International conference, Linda Lantieri observed that "reclaiming youth" is as much a movement as a methodology. Like other movements, it has an almost spiritual passion springing from the realization that one is joining a great cause. Of course, there is always a danger that idealistic zeal may cloud reason. When working with challenging youth, however, optimism is not a foolish ideal but a survival skill.

Educational researchers note the power of positive expectations with the term "Pygmalion effect", which comes from Greek mythology and George Bernard Shaw's stage play *Pygmalion*. In the musical movie version, called *My Fair Lady*, Professor Henry Higgins trains cockney girl, Eliza Doolittle, to mingle with royalty. Simply stated, optimism—or pessimism—can become a self-fulfilling prophecy.

Some scholars argue that antisocial behavior is a lifelong disorder like diabetes that can be managed but not cured. This mindset certainly would discourage an optimist. We know these kids are not easy to work with and our ability to turn them around has limits, but we prefer to face this challenge in a manner suggested by famed humanitarian Albert Schweitzer: "My knowledge is pessimistic but my willing and hoping are optimistic."[32] There is reason for hope. Research shows that inclusive schools and caring communities can develop strengths in all our children.

Former troubled youth Waln K. Brown is now an expert on resilience.[33] While speaking at a conference, he was asked, "When nothing works, how long should we keep trying?" His response was in the tradition of Winston Churchill: "Never give up. Never. Never!" Never giving up requires heroic efforts to restore troubled families. Never giving up means designing methods of inclusive discipline rather than abandoning difficult students. Never giving up means developing reclaiming interventions for violent youths rather than dumping them into the landfill of prison.

Programs that banish or warehouse our most needy students are participating in negative youth development. There are children who cannot succeed in a regular school, remain with their own families, or be served in community programs, but they still have a basic right to be raised in environments of opportunity.[34] Adults who make decisions that affect youth need to be guided by the "my child" standard: namely, every young person is entitled to the quality of care that we would expect for our own child:

> A father was being consoled at his son's funeral by friends and neighbors while his wife sobbed nearby. Their sixteen-year-old son had been the victim of a drive-by shooting. "You were a good father," said one friend, while a second offered sympathetically, "Robert was a great kid; he was a good athlete, a good student, and I'll always remember our times together volunteering at the food bank. You had a great son; I'll miss him. I'm so sorry for you and Janice; you did everything right." The father slowly turned his red-rimmed eyes toward his friend. "No," he replied, sadly shaking his head. "I didn't do everything right." He continued, as his startled friends listened, "I didn't raise the rest of the neighborhood."[35]

Zulu sociologist Herbert W. Vilakazi of South Africa calls for a return to truths that have been preserved in tribal cultures that deeply value children. He suggests that the challenges facing our children can best be overcome "when the father of the child shall be every man as old as the child's father, when the mother of the child shall be every woman as old as the child's mother; a society where the entire community is responsible."[36]

Endnotes

[1] Wolin and Wolin 1993.

[2] Seita 2000.

[3] Schulman 1952.

[4] Sampson and Laub 1993.

[5] Olweus 1993.

[6] Werner and Smith 1992.

[7] Loeber and Farrington 1998.

[8] Jason Zeidenberg of the Justice Policy Institute in Washington, D.C., collaborated with the Children and Family Justice Center of the Northwestern University School of Law to produce *Second Chances*, 1999. This is a collection of accounts of prominent citizens who were delinquents as teens but were given opportunities for rehabilitation by the juvenile justice system. Brendtro, Ness, and Mitchell describe the process by which delinquents are transformed in their book, *No Disposable Kids* (2005). A dramatic case is the boy alleged to be the arsonist responsible for the death of over ninety children and several teachers in a 1958 Chicago school fire. The Cook County Juvenile Court placed him at Starr Commonwealth where he turned his life around and went on to military service and a positive adult adjustment.

[9] Zeigarnik 1927.

[10] The stages by which people make changes in their lives, whether negative or positive, are documented by Athens 1992. Research on substance abuse done by the National Association of Addiction Treatment Providers 2000 identifies similar stages of change in the treatment process. Elsewhere, Brendtro and Ness 1983 and Larson and

Brendtro 2000 discuss the change process in psycho-educational treatment and in moral and spiritual development. Long, Fecser, and Wood 2001 extensively study how crisis can create opportunities for change.

[11] Illustrating the concept of peak experiences in transforming his own worldview, Abraham Maslow notes, "Our first baby changed me as a psychologist. It made the behaviorism I had been so enthusiastic about look so foolish that I could not stomach any more." Maslow 1971, 169.

[12] Peck 1978, 1.

[13] Quirk 2000, 1.

[14] Coles 1990.

[15] Lantieri 2001.

[16] Mendler and Curwin 1999.

[17] Laursen 2000. Brendtro, Ness, and Mitchell 2005. Vorrath and Brendtro 1985.

[18] Gibbs, Potter, and Goldstein 1995.

[19] Long, Fecser, and Wood 2001.

[20] Edelstien 1990.

[21] Cohen 1998.

[22] Lober 1991, 396.

[23] Lay 2000.

[24] Gold and Osgood 1992.

[25] Coopersmith 1967.

[26] Brendtro and Bacon 1995.

[27] Giacobbe, Traynellis-Yurek, and Laursen 1999.

[28] Coles 1990, 309.

[29] Fromm 1998.

[30] Kuykendal 1992.

[31] Cited in Ellen Key 1909, 107.

[32] Schweitzer 1955.

[33] Brown 1994.

[34] Brendtro and Cunningham 1998.

[35] Baines and Seita 1999, 29.

[36] Vilakazi 1993.

Bibliography

Addams, Jane. 1909. *The Spirit of Youth and the City Streets*. New York: Macmillan.

Adler, Alfred. 1930. *The Education of Children*. South Bend, IN: George Allen and Unwin, Ltd.

Aichhorn, August. 1935. *Wayward Youth*. New York: Viking Press.

Allen, J., and D. Land. 1999. Attachment in Adolescence. In *Handbook of Attachment*, edited by J. Cassidy and P. Shaver, 319–335. New York: Guilford Press.

Allers, Rudolph. 1934. *Practical Psychology in Character Development*. London: Sheed and Ward.

American Psychiatric Association. 1994. *Diagnostic and Statistical Manual of Mental Disorders, 4th ed. (DSM-IV)*. Washington D.C.: American Psychiatric Association.

Anderson, E. 1994. The Code of the Streets. *Atlantic Monthly* 273 (5): 80–94.

Athens, Lonnie. 1992. *The Creation of Dangerous Violent Criminals*. Urbana, IL: University of Illinois Press.

Azar, Beth. 1998. Split Second Evaluations Shape Our Moods, Actions. *APA Monitor* 29 (9): 13.

Baines, Tyrone, and John Seita. 1999. Raising the Rest of the Neighborhood. *Reclaiming Children and Youth* 8 (1): 25–29.

Balswick, J. O., and C. Macrides. 1975. Parental Stimulus for Adolescent Rebellion. *Adolescence* 10:253–256.

Bandura, Albert. 1982. The Psychology of Chance Encounters and Life Paths. *American Psychologist* 27 (7): 47–55.

Bandura, Albert. 1986. *Social Foundations of Thought and Action: A Cognitive Theory*. Englewood Cliffs, NJ: Prentice Hall.

Barkley, R. A., G. H. Edwards, and A. L. Robin. 1999. *Defiant Teens*. New York: Guilford Press.

Beck, Aaron T. 1999. *Prisoners of Hate: The Cognitive Basis of Anger, Hostility, and Violence*. New York: HarperCollins Publishers.

Benard, Bonnie. 1997. Fostering Resiliency in Urban Schools. In *Closing the Achievement Gap*, edited by B. Williams. Alexandria, VA: ASCD.

Benson, Peter. 1997. *All Kids Are Our Kids: What Communities Must Do to Raise Caring and Responsible Children and Adolescents*. San Francisco: Jossey-Bass.

Blom, G., B. Cheney, and J. Snoddy. 1986. *Stress in Childhood: An Intervention Model for Teachers and Other Professionals*. New York: Columbia University.

Bowlby, John 1982. *Attachment and Loss*. New York: Basic Books.

Braithwaite, John 1989. *Crime, Shame, and Reintegration*. Cambridge: Cambridge University Press.

Branden, N. 1994. *Six Pillars of Self-Esteem*. New York: Bantam Books.

Brendtro, Larry. 1965. *Verbal and Conceptual Factors in Preadolescence with Impaired Relationship Capacity*. Ph.D. diss., University of Michigan.

Brendtro, Larry, and Joan Bacon. 1995. Youth Empowerment and Teamwork. In *Teamwork Models and Experience in Education*, edited by H. Garner, 55–72. Boston: Allyn and Bacon.

Brendtro, Larry, Martin Brokenleg, and Steve Van Bockern. 2002. *Reclaiming Youth at Risk: Our Hope for the Future*, (Rev. Ed.). Bloomington, IN: Solution Tree (formerly National Educational Service).

Brendtro, Larry, and James Cunningham. 1998. Meeting the Developmental Needs of Incarcerated Youth. *Reclaiming Children and Youth* 7 (2): 104–109.

Brendtro, Larry, and Lesley du Toit. 2005. *Response Ability Pathways. Restoring Bonds of Respect*. Cape Town: Pretext Publishers.

Brendtro, Larry, and Arlin Ness. 1983. *Re-educating Troubled Youth*. New York: Aldine de Gruyter.

Brendtro, Larry, and Arlin Ness. 1995. Fixing Flaws or Building Strengths? *Reclaiming Children and Youth* 4 (2): 2–7.

Brendtro, Larry, Arlin Ness, and Martin Mitchell. 2005. *No Disposable Kids*. Bloomington, IN: Solution Tree (formerly National Educational Service).

Brendtro, Larry, and Mary Shahbazian. 2004. *Troubled Children and Youth: Turning Problems Into Opportunities*. Champaign, IL: Research Press.

Brokenleg, Martin, Steve Van Bockern, and Larry Brendtro. 1999. Raising Respectful Kids. *Reclaiming Children and Youth* 8 (1): 2–6.

Bronfenbrenner, Urie. 1979. *The Ecology of Human Development*. Cambridge, MA: Harvard University Press.

———. 1986. Alienation and the Four Worlds of Childhood. *Phi Delta Kappan* 67:430–436.

Brown, Lynn M., and Carol Gilligan. 1992. *Meeting at the Crossroads*. Cambridge, MA: Harvard University Press.

Brown, Waln K. 1983. *The Other Side of Delinquency*. New Brunswick, NJ: Rutgers University Press.

———. 1994. *The Other Side of Delinquency*. Cameron, WV: William Gladden Foundation.

———. 1997. Education and Delinquency Devolution: A Case History. *Reclaiming Children and Youth* 6 (1): 34–37.

Buford, Bill, ed. 1955. *The Family*. New York: Granta Books.

Burns, J. M. 1988. *Leadership*. New York: Harper and Row.

Callahan, Steve. 1986. *Adrift: Seventy-Six Days Lost at Sea*. New York: Ballantine Books.

Chambers, J. C. 2000. Unmasking the Terror. *Reclaiming Children and Youth* 9 (1): 14–16.

Clark, A. 1998. *Defense Mechanisms in the Counseling Process*. Thousand Oaks, CA: Sage.

Cohen, M. B. 1998. Perceptions of Power in Client/Worker Relationships. *Families in Society* 79 (4): 433–442.

Cohler, B. 1987. Adversity, Resilience, and the Study of Lives. In *The Invulnerable Child*, edited by E. J. Anthony and B. J. Cohler, 363–424. New York: Guilford Press.

Coles, Robert. 1990. *The Spiritual Life of Children*. Boston: Houghton-Mifflin.

Coopersmith, Stanley. 1967. *The Antecedents of Self-Esteem*. San Francisco: W. H. Freeman and Company.

Covey, Stephen R. 1990. *The Seven Habits of Highly Effective People*. New York: Fireside.

Damon, Matt, and Ben Affleck. 1997. *Good Will Hunting: A Screenplay*. New York: Miramax/Hyperion.

Dedman, Bill. 2000. Examining the Actions of an Adolescent Killer. In *"Deadly Lessons: School Shooters Tell Why." Chicago Sun-Times*, 16–20 October, exclusive report, 7–9.

Docherty, J. P. 2000. Presentation to the Brown Schools, 19 April at Sand Point, Idaho.

Dodge, K. A. 1993. Social Cognitive Mechanisms in the Development of Conduct Disorder and Depression. *Annual Review of Psychology* 44:559–584.

Dreikurs, R. 1964. *Children of the Challenge*. New York: Hawthorn.

DuBeau, Tania. 1997. Survival and Sexual Identity: Calvin, a Gay Adolescent. *Reclaiming Children and Youth* 6 (1): 22–25.

Durkin, Robert. 1988. Restructuring for Competence: A Case for the Democratization and Communitization of Children's Programs. In *Challenging the Limits of Care*, edited by R. Small and F. Alwon. Needham, MA: Albert E. Trieschman Center.

Dwyer, K., D. Osher, and W. Warger. 1998. *Early Warning, Timely Response: A Guide to Safe Schools*. Washington, DC: United States Department of Education (ERIC document #ED 418 372).

Edelstien, M. Gerald. 1990. *Symptom Analysis: A Method of Brief Therapy*. New York: W. W. Norton.

Edwards, Rose Maria. 1991. *A. S. Makarenko's General Education Ideas and Their Applicability to a Nontotalitarian Society*. Ann Arbor, MI: University Microfilms International.

Eisner, E. 1990. Who Decides What Schools Teach? *Phi Delta Kappan* 71:523–526.

Erickson, Milton. 1980. Pediatric Hypnotherapy. In *The Collected Papers of Milton H. Erickson on Hypnosis*, edited by E. L. Rossi, vol. 4. New York: Irvington.

Erikson, Erik. 1950. *Childhood and Society*. New York: Norton.

Everson, Tom. 1994. Resilience and Skill-Building: A Spiritual Perspective. *Journal of Emotional and Behavioral Problems* 3 (2): 25–29.

Farrelly, F., and J. Brandsma. 1974. *Provocative Therapy*. Cupertino, CA: Meta Publications, Inc.

Fine, Michelle. 1993. Making Controversy: Who's at Risk? In *Children At Risk in America*, edited by R. Wolins, 91–110. Albany, NY: Albany State University Press.

Finkelhor, David. 1979. *Sexually Victimized Children*. New York: Free Press.

Freado, Mark. 2001. *Problems as Opportunity*. Video presentation at the Black Hills Seminars, 1 July, in Rapid City, SD.

Freire, Paulo. 1970. *Pedagogy of the Oppressed*. New York: Seabury Press.

Freud, Sigmund. [1913] 1958. The Beginning of Treatment. In *Standard Edition of the Complete Psychological Works of Sigmund Freud*, edited by J. Strachey. London: Hogarth Press.

Fromm, Erika. 1998. Lost and Found Half a Century Later: Letters by Freud and Einstein. *American Psychologist* 53 (110): 1195–1198.

Garbarino, James. 1999. *Lost Boys*. New York: The Free Press.

Garmezy, N. 1983. Foreword to *Vulnerable but Invincible: A Longitudinal Study of Resilient Children and Youth*, edited by E. Werner and R. S. Smith. New York: McGraw Hill.

Gaston, L. 1991. Reliability and Criterion-Related Validity of the California Psychotherapy Alliance Scales—Patient Version. *Psychological Assessment* 3:68–74.

Giacobbe, George, Elaine Traynellis-Yurek, and Erik Laursen. 1999. *Strength-Based Strategies for Children and Youth: An Annotated Bibliography.* Richmond, VA: G & T Publishing.

Gibbs, John, Granville Bud Potter, and Arnold Goldstein. 1995. *The EQUIP Program.* Champaign, IL: Research Press.

Gibbs, John, Granville Bud Potter, Arnold Goldstein, and Larry Brendtro. 1998. How EQUIP Programs Help Youth Change. *Reclaiming Children and Youth* 7 (2): 117–122.

Gilligan, James 1997. *Violence: Reflections on a National Epidemic.* New York: Random House.

Gold, Martin, and D. Wayne Osgood. 1992. *Personality and Peer Influence in Juvenile Corrections.* Westport, CT: Greenwood Press.

Goldstein, A., K. Heller, and Lee B. Sechrest. 1966. *Psychotherapy and the Psychology of Behavior Change.* New York: John Wiley and Sons.

Good Will Hunting. 1997. Produced by Lawrence Bender. Directed by Gus Van Sant. 126 min. Miramax. Videocassette.

Greenspan, S., and C. Cullander. 1975. A Systematic Metapsychological Assessment of the Course of Analysis. *Journal of the American Psychoanalytic Association* 23:107–108.

Guarino-Ghezzi, Susan, Kim Godfrey, and Paul Bankowski. 1997. Making Peace Between Cops and Kids. *Reclaiming Children and Youth* 6 (3): 182–184.

Haley, Jay. 1973. *Uncommon Therapy: The Psychiatric Techniques of Milton H. Erickson, M.D.* New York: Norton.

Henry, W. P., T. E. Schacht, and H. H. Strupp. 1986. Structural Analysis of Social Behavior: Application to a Study of Interpersonal Process of Differential Therapeutic Outcome. *Journal of Consulting and Clinical Psychology* 54:27–31.

Hobbs, Nicholas. 1994. *The Troubled and Troubling Child*. Cleveland, OH: American Re-Education Association.

Hoffer, W. 1949. Deceiving the Deceiver. In *Searchlights on Delinquency*, edited by K. R. Eissler, 150–155. New York: International Universities Press.

Horvath, A., L. Gaston, and L. Luborsky. 1993. The Therapeutic Alliance and Its Measures. In *Psychodynamic Treatment Research*, edited by N. Miller, L. Luborsky, J. Barber, and J. P. Docherty, 247–273. New York: Basic Books.

Hubble, Mark A., Barry L. Duncan, and Scott D. Miller. 1999. *The Heart and Soul of Change*. Washington, DC: American Psychological Association.

Huey, S., S. Hengeler, M. Brondino, and S. Pickrel. 2000. Mechanisms of Change in Multisystemic Therapy: Reducing Delinquent Behavior Through Therapist Adherence and Improved Family and Peer Functioning. *Journal of Consulting and Clinical Psychology* 68 (3): 451–467.

Hyman, Irwin. 2000. Dangerous Schools/Dangerous Students: Defining and Assessing Student Alienation Syndrome. Paper presented at OSEP Research Project Director's Conference, 13 July, in Washington, D.C.

Hyman, Irwin, and Pamela Snook. 1999. *Dangerous Schools: What We Can Do About the Physical and Emotional Abuse of Our Children*. San Francisco: Jossey-Bass.

Jacobs, Don. 1995. Lost Youth or Criminals? *Caring* 10 (4): 11–13.

James, William. 1913. *Notations from Talks to Teachers on Psychology and to Students on Some of Life's Ideals*. New York: Henry Holt and Company.

Kellerman, Jonathan. 1999. *Savage Spawn: Reflections on Violent Children*. New York: Ballantine.

Key, Ellen. 1909. *The Century of the Child*. New York: G. P. Putnam and Sons.

Knitzer, Jane, Zina Steinberg, and Brahm Fleisch. 1990. *At the Schoolhouse Door*. New York: Bank Street College of Education.

Korczak, Janusz. 1901. *Children of the Streets*. New York: G. P. Putnam and Sons.

Kounin, J. S. 1970. *Discipline and Group Management in Classrooms*. New York: Holt, Rinehart, and Winston.

Kuykendal, Crystal. 1992. *Reclaiming Black and Hispanic Students*. Bloomington, IN: Solution Tree (formerly National Educational Service).

Lantieri, Linda. 2001. *Schools with Spirit*. Boston: Beacon Press.

Larson, R. 2000. Toward a Psychology of Positive Youth Development. *American Psychologist* 55 (1): 170–183.

Larson, Scott, and Larry Brendtro. 2000. *Reclaiming Our Prodigal Sons and Daughters*. Bloomington, IN: Solution Tree (formerly National Educational Service).

Laursen, Erik. 2000. Strength-Based Practice with Children in Trouble. *Reclaiming Children and Youth* 9 (2): 70–75.

Lay, Jonathan. 2000. The Person Behind the File Number. *Reclaiming Children and Youth* 9 (2): 68–69.

Levy, E. 1937. Primary Affect Hunger. *American Journal of Psychiatry* 94:643–652.

Lewis, Michael. 1997. *Altering Fate: Why the Past Does Not Predict the Future*. New York: The Guilford Press.

Lhotzky, Stephan. 1994. Karl Wilker's Lindenhof. *Journal of Emotional and Behavioral Problems* 3 (2): 53–55.

Lober, R. 1991. Anti-Social Behavior: More Enduring Than Changeable? *Journal of American Academy of Child and Adolescent Psychiatry* 30 (3): 393–396.

Loeber, R., and D. P. Farrington. 1998. *Serious and Violent Juvenile Offenders*. Thousand Oaks, CA: Sage.

Long, Nicholas, Frank Fecser, and Larry Brendtro. 1998. Life Space Crisis Intervention: New Skills for Reclaiming Students Showing Patterns of Self-Defeating Behavior. *Healing* 3 (2): 2–22.

Long, Nicholas, Frank Fecser, and Mary M. Wood. 2001. *Life Space Crisis Intervention*. Austin, TX: PRO-ED.

Maag, John W. 1996. *Parenting without Punishment*. Philadelphia, PA: The Charles Press Publishers.

Makarenko, Anton. 1976. *Anton Makarenko: His Life and Work in Education*. Moscow, USSR: Progress Press.

Males, Michael. 1996. *The Scapegoat Generation*. Monroe, ME: Courage Press.

Martin, D. J., J. P. Garske, and M. K. Davis. 2000. Relation of Therapeutic Alliance with Outcome and Other Variables: A Meta-Analytic Review. *Journal of Consulting and Clinical Psychology* 68 (3): 438–450.

Maslow, Abraham H. 1971. *The Farther Reaches of Human Nature*. New York: The Viking Press.

Masterson, J. F. 1985. *Real Self*. New York: Brunner/Mazel.

Matthews, S. 1995. Juvenile Capital Offenders on Empathy. *Reclaiming Children and Youth* 4 (2): 10–12.

McCord, W., and J. McCord. 1956. *Psychopathy and Delinquency*. New York: Grune and Stratton.

McIntosh, Peggy. 1995. White Privilege and Male Privilege: A Personal Account of Coming to See Correspondences Through Work in Women's Studies. In *Race, Class, and Gender*, edited by Margaret L. Andersen and Patricia Hill Collins, 76–87. Belmont, CA: Wadsworth.

McIntyre, T. 1996. Earning the Respect of Streetwise Youngsters. *Reclaiming Children and Youth* 38 (4): 38–41.

Mendler, Allen, and Richard Curwin. 1999. *Discipline with Dignity for Challenging Youth*. Bloomington, IN: Solution Tree (formerly National Educational Service).

Menninger, Karl. 1963. *The Vital Balance: The Life Process in Mental Health and Illness*. New York: The Viking Press.

Miller, Walter. 1958. Lower-Class Culture as a Generating Milieu of Gang Delinquency. *Journal of Social Issues* 14 (3): 5–19.

Montgomery, Michael. 1997. The Powerlessness of Punishment: Angry Pride and Delinquent Identity. *Reclaiming Children and Youth* 6 (3): 162–166.

National Association of Addiction Treatment Providers (NAATP). 2000. Motivating Alcoholics to Seek Treatment Without Confrontation. *Behavioral Health Care Tomorrow* 9 (2): 32.

Newman, Barbara, and Philip Newman. 1986. *Adolescent Development*. Columbus, OH: Merrill Publishing Company.

Newman, R. P., S. M. Smith, and R. Murphy. 1998. *A Matter of Money: The Cost and Financing of Youth Development*. Washington, DC: Academy for Educational Development.

Odney, John, and Larry Brendtro. 1992. Students Grade Their Schools. *Journal of Emotional and Behavioral Problems* 2 (1): 4–8.

Olweus, Dan. 1993. *Bullying at School: What We Know and What We Can Do*. Denver, CO: Blackwell Press.

Olweus, Dan. 2000. Personal communication with the author, June.

Palmer, T. 1974. *The Youth Authority's Community Treatment Project*. Sacramento, CA: California Youth Authority. March.

Paragament, K. 1997. *The Psychology of Religion and Coping*. New York: Guilford Press.

Patterson, G. R., and M. S. Fopgatch. 1998. Therapist Behavior as a Determinant for Client Noncompliance: A Paradox for the Behavior Modifier. *Journal of Consulting and Clinical Psychology* 53:846–857.

Patterson, G. R., J. B. Reid, and T. J. Dishion. 1992. *A Social Interactional Approach: Antisocial Boys*. Eugene, OR: Castalia Press.

Peck, M. Scott. 1978. *The Road Less Traveled*. New York: Simon and Schuster.

Pittman, K., and M. Irby. 1996. *Preventing Problems or Promoting Development: Competing Priorities or Inseparable Goals?* International Youth Foundation. Internet article at www.iyfnet.org/programs/preventingprob.html.

Pollack, W. 1998. *Real Boys: Rescuing Our Sons from the Myths of Boyhood*. New York: Henry Holt.

Quirk, Constance. 2000. The Significance of the Past. *Developmentions*. University of Georgia, Athens: Newsletter of the Developmental Therapy-Teaching Programs, 1. Spring.

Rapaport, Anatol. 1960. *Fights, Games, and Debates*. Ann Arbor: University of Michigan Press.

Raychaba, Brian. 1992. Doing and Being Done To. *Journal of Emotional and Behavioral Problems* 1 (3): 4–9.

Reclaiming Youth International. 2000. *The Developmental Audit Training Process*. Sioux Falls, SD: Augustana College. [Note: Developmental Audit is a trademark of Reclaiming Youth International, which provides training and certification in this process.]

Redl, Fritz. 1966. *When We Deal with Children*. New York: The Free Press.

Rhodes, R. 1999. *The Discoveries of a Maverick Criminologist*. New York: Alfred A. Knopf.

Rhodes, Warren, and Kim Hoey. 1994. *Overcoming Childhood Misfortune: Children Who Beat the Odds*. Westport, CT: Praeger.

Roberts, Monty. 1996. *The Man Who Listens to Horses*. New York: Random House.

Rutter, M., H. Giller, and A. Hagell. 1998. *Antisocial Behavior by Young People*. Boston: Cambridge University Press.

Safran, J. D., P. Crocker, S. McMain, and P. Murray. 1990. The Therapeutic Alliance Rupture as a Therapy Event for Empirical Investigation. *Psychotherapy*, 27: 154–165.

Safran, Jeremy D., and J. Christopher Muran. 2000. *Negotiating the Therapeutic Alliance*. New York: The Guilford Press.

Sampson, R. J., and J. H. Laub. 1993. *Crime in the Making: Pathways and Turning Points*. Cambridge, MA: Harvard University Press.

Schorr, Lisbeth. 1989. *Within Our Reach*. New York: Anchor.

Schulman, Irving. 1952. Delinquents. In *The Fields of Group Psychotherapy*, edited by S. R. Slavson, 196–214. New York: John Wiley & Sons.

Schultz, Theodore. 1974. Marriage, Family Human Capital, and Fertility. Cited in James Traub, What No School Can Do. *New York Times Sunday Magazine*, 16 January 2000.

Schwartz, Ira. 1989. *(In)Justice for Juveniles*. Lexington, MA: D. C. Heath and Company.

Schweitzer, Albert. 1955. *Out of My Life and Thought*. New York: Henry Holt.

Seita, John. 1994. Resiliency From the Other Side of the Desk. *Journal of Emotional and Behavioral Problems* 3 (2): 15–18.

Seita, John. 2000. *God Is in the Kitchen and Other Everyday Miracles: A Daughter's Gift and a Daddy's Love*. Lincoln, NE: iUniverse.

Seita, John, Martin Mitchell, and Christi Tobin. 1996. *In Whose Best Interest? One Child's Odyssey, A Nation's Responsibility*. Elizabethtown, PA: Continental Press.

Skinner, B. F. 1989. *Recent Issues in the Analysis of Behavior*. Columbus, OH: Merrill.

St. Augustine. [1923] 1959. *The Confessions of St. Augustine*. London: Fontana Books.

Taylor, Jill McLean, Carol Gilligan, and Amy M. Sullivan. 1996. What Gets Me in Trouble is "My Big Mouth!!" Women and Girls, Race and Relationship. *Reclaiming Children and Youth* 5 (2): 68–73.

Treischman, Al, James Whittaker, and Larry Brendtro. 1969. *The Other 23 Hours*. Chicago: Aldine.

Tutu, Desmond. 1999. *No Future Without Forgiveness*. New York: Doubleday.

U.S. Department of Justice. 2000. FBI File number MP282-0, January 10. Re: Camilla B. (deceased).

Vilakazi, Herbert W. 1993. Rediscovering Lost Truths. *Journal of Emotional and Behavioral Problems* 1 (4): 37.

Vorrath, Harry, and Larry Brendtro. 1985. *Positive Peer Culture*, 2d ed. Hawthorne, NY: Aldine de Gruyter.

Way, Daniel W. 1993. I Just Have a Half Heart. *Journal of Emotional and Behavioral Problems* 2 (1): 4–5.

Werner, Emmy, and Ruth S. Smith. 1977. *Kauai's Children Come of Age*. Honolulu: University of Hawaii Press.

———. 1992. *Overcoming the Odds: High Risk Children from Birth to Adulthood*. Ithaca, NY: Cornell University Press.

Winnicott, D. W. 1949. Hate in the Countertransference. *International Journal of Psychoanalysis*, 30:69–74.

Wolin, Steven J., and Sybil Wolin. 1993. *The Resilient Self*. New York: Villard.

Wood, Mary M., Larry Brendtro, Frank Fecser, and Polly Nichols. 1999. *Psychoeducation, An Idea Whose Time Has Come*. Reston, VA: Council for Children with Behavioral Disorders.

Zeidenberg, Jason. 1999. *Second Chances*. Washington, D.C.: Justice Policy Institute.

Zeidner, M., and N. Endler 1995. *Handbook of Coping*. New York: Allyn and Bacon.

Zeigarnik, Bluma. 1927. Das Behalten von erledigten und unerledigten Handlungen (The memory of completed and uncompleted tasks). *Psychologische Forschung* 9:1–85.

Strength-Based Training Opportunities

Training With Author John Seita

John Seita provides research-based training and professional development. His research on youth at risk is blended with his own gritty real-world experience and scholarship to provide the very best training on how to understand and reclaim all youth. All training sessions are designed to build the capacity of those who work with challenging youth to be more effective in understanding and reclaiming them.

- *Family Privilege and Loss: A Culture of Privileges and Disadvantages Explored* examines how a lack of family stability can affect classrooms, residential settings, and programs.

- *The Circle of Courage: Courage for the Discouraged* uses the research of Brendtro and Brokenleg to explore ways of tapping the potentials of even the most discouraged youth.

- *From Risk to Resilience: Connectedness, Continuity, Dignity, and Opportunity for Youth Development* provides practitioners with a straightforward framework for practicing positive youth development with young people who are at risk.

- *Transforming from the Pessimistic Lens to the Opportunity Lens* provides 12 ways to move from rejecting to reclaiming kids.

- *Problems as Opportunities* considers a range of alternatives for reaching challenging children and youth.

- *Kids Who Outwit Adults: Understanding the Private Logic of Defiance* draws upon Dr. Seita's own experience to expose the thinking behind the behaviors of adult-wary and angry youth.

- *In Whose Best Interest?* communicates Dr. Seita's own experience to provide a blueprint for success with challenging youth.

For further information contact John Seita:

Phone: 269-501-5487 • E-mail: john.seita@comcast.net
Web Site: www.johnseita.net/index.html

Comprehensive Training

No Disposable Kids® offers a range of strength-based training curriculums:

- *Building Safe and Reclaiming Schools* prevents conflict and manages crisis.

- *Uniting Humankind* is an experiential program designed for healing racism.

- *Cultivating Respectful Environments* targets bullying and uses core training in Response Ability Pathways (RAP) to form respectful bonds and group climates.

Reclaiming Youth conducts *Reclaiming Youth Seminars* in the U.S. and Canada and publishes the quarterly journal *Reclaiming Children and Youth*. It also operates a Web-based bookstore and the Reclaiming Youth Speakers Bureau. Reclaiming Youth's mission is based on the Circle of Courage with Response Ability Pathways (RAP) providing core training in this approach.

Basic Training in Building Strengths

Response Ability Pathways (RAP) provides essential "basic training" for all who deal with young persons in family, school, or community settings. Children and youth need supportive persons who *respond* to their needs rather than *react* to their problems. RAP provides these *response-abilities* which enable one to guide young persons on *pathways to responsibility*.

- *RAP applies Circle of Courage principles to meet growth needs of all young persons.* The goal is to provide children with opportunities to develop belonging, mastery, independence, and generosity.

- *RAP methods are grounded in research evidence* on resilience, brain science, and positive youth development.[1, 2]

- *RAP provides a powerful alternative to both punitive and permissive approaches.* Instead of reactive, coercive interactions, young persons are enlisted as responsible agents in positive change. RAP deals with problems by focusing on strengths and solutions. Rather than enforcing obedience, RAP sets high expectations for youth to take responsibility and show respect for themselves and others.

- *RAP taps and develops the innate strength and resilience of young persons.* The course focuses on three interventions: *Connect, Clarify,* and *Restore.* These are the normal "abilities" of the resilient human brain.

- *RAP is highly experiential and provides practical skills for building courageous kids.* Basic RAP principles are presented in creative formats, and the course is enlivened by engaging videos and small-group role plays.

- *RAP is useful for all who are concerned with youth, whether professionals or lay persons.* This course is well-received by educators, counselors, social workers, psychologists, youth workers, and staff in treatment and juvenile justice settings. Training also can include parents, foster parents, mentors, and mature youth who are peer helpers. Training leads to RAP certification, and course credit can be arranged.

For further information contact:

No Disposable Kids
Phone: 1-800-315-5640
E-mail: info@ndk.org
Web Site: www.ndk.org

Reclaiming Youth
Phone: 1-800-647-5244
E-mail: courage@reclaiming.com
Web Site: www.reclaiming.com

---

[1]Brendtro, Larry, and Lesley du Toit. 2005. *Response Ability Pathways* [RAP]. Cape Town: Pretext Publishers.

[2]Brendtro, Larry, Arlin Ness, and Martin Mitchell. 2005. *No disposable kids.* Bloomington, IN: Solution Tree (formerly National Educational Service).

Make the Most of Your Professional Development Investment

Let Solution Tree (formerly National Educational Service) schedule time for you and your staff with leading practitioners in the areas of:

- **Professional Learning Communities** with Richard DuFour, Robert Eaker, Rebecca DuFour, and associates
- **Effective Schools** with associates of Larry Lezotte
- **Assessment for Learning** with Rick Stiggins and associates
- **Crisis Management and Response** with Cheri Lovre
- **Classroom Management** with Lee Canter and associates
- **Discipline With Dignity** with Richard Curwin and Allen Mendler
- **PASSport to Success** (parental involvement) with Vickie Burt
- **Peacemakers** (violence prevention) with Jeremy Shapiro

Additional presentations are available in the following areas:

- At-Risk Youth Issues
- Bullying Prevention/Teasing and Harassment
- Team Building and Collaborative Teams
- Data Collection and Analysis
- Embracing Diversity
- Literacy Development
- Motivating Techniques for Staff and Students

Solution Tree

304 West Kirkwood Avenue
Bloomington, IN 47404-5131
(812) 336-7700
(800) 733-6786 (toll free)
FAX (812) 336-7790
e-mail: info@solution-tree.com
www.solution-tree.com

NEED MORE COPIES OR ADDITIONAL RESOURCES ON THIS TOPIC?

Need more copies of this book? Want your own copy? Need additional resources on this topic? If so, you can order additional materials by using this form or by calling us toll free at (800) 733-6786 or (812) 336-7700. Or you can order by FAX at (812) 336-7790, or visit our web site at www.solution-tree.com.

Title	Price*	Quantity	Total
Kids Who Outwit Adults	$ 24.95		
No Disposable Kids	24.95		
The Resilience Revolution	24.95		
Peacemakers: A Violence Prevention Program	169.00		
Reclaiming Youth at Risk (revised edition)	23.95		
Reclaiming Youth at Risk (audio book on 4 CDs)	29.95		
Reclaiming Youth at Risk (video set)	295.00		
Reclaiming Our Prodigal Sons and Daughters	18.95		
Reclaiming Our Prodigal Sons and Daughters CD-ROM	39.95		
Teaching Empathy	34.95		
SUBTOTAL			
SHIPPING Continental U.S.: Please add 6% of order total. Outside continental U.S.: Please add 8% of order total.			
HANDLING Continental U.S.: Please add $4. Outside continental U.S.: Please add $6.			
TOTAL (U.S. funds)			

*Price subject to change without notice.

❏ Check enclosed   ❏ Purchase order enclosed
❏ Money order   ❏ VISA, MasterCard, Discover, or American Express (circle one)

Credit Card No._____ Exp. Date_____
Cardholder Signature _____

SHIP TO:

First Name_____ Last Name_____
Position _____
Institution Name_____
Address_____
City_____ State_____ ZIP_____
Phone_____ FAX_____
E-mail _____

Solution Tree (formerly National Educational Service)
304 West Kirkwood Avenue
Bloomington, IN 47404-5131
(812) 336-7700 • (800) 733-6786 (toll free)
FAX (812) 336-7790
e-mail: orders@solution-tree.com • www.solution-tree.com